Tunisia

by Peter Lilley

After working as a local newspaper journalist
and radio reporter, Peter Lilley became a
full-time travel writer in 1983. He first visited
Tunisia three years later and has made
regular trips ever since. Specialising in
North Africa and the Far East, he has
contributed to many newspapers and
magazines and is an almost weekly
contributor to the *Travel Trade Gazette*.

Above: *camels arriving at the Festival du Sahara, Douz*

AA Publishing

Local women shopping in the market at Houmt Souq

Written by Peter Lilley

First published 2000
Reprinted Feb and Aug 2000; Feb 2001; May 2002;
April 2003
Reprinted 2004. Information verified and updated.
Reprinted Jul and Dec 2004
Reprinted Feb and Aug 2005.
Reprinted Apr 2006
Reprinted Feb and May 2007

© Automobile Association Developments Limited 2004
Maps © Automobile Association Developments Limited
2000

Published by AA Publishing, a trading name of Automobile
Association Developments Limited, whose registered
office is Fanum House, Basing View, Basingstoke,
Hampshire RG21 4EA. Registered number 1878835.

Find out more about
AA Publishing and the
wide range of travel
publications and services
the AA provides by
visiting our web site at
www.theAA.com/travel

A03454

Colour separation: Chroma Graphics (Overseas) Pte Ltd,
Singapore
Printed and bound in Italy by Printer Trento S.r.l.

Contents

About this Book

KEY TO SYMBOLS

🗺 map reference to the maps found in the What to See section

✉ address or location

☎ telephone number

🕐 opening times

🍴 restaurant or café on premises or near by

Ⓜ nearest underground train station

🚌 nearest bus/tram route

🚃 nearest overground train station

🛳 ferry crossings and boat excursions

✈ travel by air

ℹ tourist information

♿ facilities for visitors with disabilities

✋ admission charge

↔ other places of interest near by

❓ other practical information

➤ indicates the page where you will find a fuller description

---

This book is divided into five sections to cover the most important aspects of your visit to Tunisia.

Viewing Tunisia pages 5–14
An introduction to Tunisia by the author.
  Tunisia's Features
  Essence of Tunisia
  The Shaping of Tunisia
  Peace and Quiet
  Tunisia's Famous

Top Ten pages 15–26
The author's choice of the Top Ten places to see in Tunisia, each with practical information.

What to See pages 27–90
The five main areas of Tunisia, each with its own brief introduction and an alphabetical listing of the main attractions.
  Practical information
  Snippets of 'Did you know…' information
  3 suggested walks
  4 suggested tours
  2 features

Where To… pages 91–116
Detailed listings of the best places to eat, stay, shop, take the children and be entertained.

Practical Matters pages 117–24
A highly visual section containing essential travel information.

Maps
All map references are to the individual maps found in the What to See section of this guide.

For example, El Jem has the reference
🗺 28C5 – indicating the page on which the map is located and the grid square in which the amphitheatre is to be found. A list of the maps that have been used in this travel guide can be found in the index.

Prices
Where appropriate, an indication of the cost of an establishment is given by **£** signs:
£££ denotes higher prices, **££** denotes average prices, while **£** denotes lower charges.

Star Ratings
Most of the places described in this book have been given a separate rating:

❂❂❂ Do not miss
❂❂ Highly recommended
❂ Worth seeing

Viewing
Tunisia

Above: *An ancient mosque above the abandoned village of Douiret*
Right: *Sweet-smelling jasmine offered in Hammamet*

5

Peter Lilley's Tunisia

Inset: *A médina door studded with patterns and symbols*
Below: *Men intent on a game of draughts*

Tunisia is a mainstream Mediterranean holiday destination but it still attracts a lot of first-time visitors. In unfamiliar surroundings there is always the temptation to be cautious, trusting that the land and its people will reveal themselves in their own time: with Tunisia the secret is to immerse oneself in the culture from the moment of arrival.

If there's a choice, pick one of the early summer months and go to one of the major centres such as Tunis, Sousse or Sfax. Drop the bags and venture straight out into the streets in the late afternoon, the most magical time of day. Tunisians are at their most animated and convivial in the early evening, having been up since sunrise or soon after, and there is an infectious gaiety in the air, a sense that whatever fortunes have been won or lost, the day is over. On every street corner and scrap of rough ground, boys kick footballs and in the smoky bars and cafés this is the time for coffee, cards, chatter and *chichas* with perhaps a bottle of Celtia, Tunisia's only beer.

In the mysterious *médinas*, where skinny cats slink into every corner and there is the feeling that a thousand secrets seem to lurk behind every studded door, shops and stalls in the *souqs* and surrounding streets spring to life to serve the homeward bound with the freshest food. Chickens are butchered to order, fish are only minutes out of the sea, bread is baked on the spot and stacks of colourful vegetables are haggled over with shouts and handshakes.

Tunisia's Features

A tradtional Bedouin band tunes up for a desert festival

Geography
• Tunisia is the northernmost country in Africa; it lies just 80km southwest of Sicily. It measures 750km from north to south but only 150km from west to east, making it slightly larger than the US state of Florida.
• The northern and eastern coastlines are bordered by the Mediterranean, while much of the southern half of the country is within the Sahara Desert.

Climate
• Summers are hot and dry. In July and August daytime temperatures on the east coast average 30°C with 12 hours of sunshine; in the desert it can reach 45°C.
• In the north, winters are mild but quite wet with occasional snow.
• Daytime temperatures in the south average 20°C but fall rapidly at night to near freezing.

People
• Tunisia has a population of around 10 million.
• More than half the population is under 18 and more than 30 per cent under 14.
• About 99 per cent of the population are Muslim with tiny Christian and Jewish minorities.
•Tunisian women enjoy considerable freedom when compared with other Muslim countries, though many older women still choose to wear the veil.

Language
• Arabic is the official language but almost everyone speaks some French.
• It is rare to find English or German spoken outside the main beach resorts.

The Berbers
The Berbers have been found in various parts of North Africa since *c*2000 BC and are generally considered to be the original Tunisians. A few centres of Berber culture survive in southern Tunisia where the people still speak the Berber language and are noted for their colourful dress, beautiful jewellery and weavings, and intricate woodcarving.

7

Essence of Tunisia

Until now, most visitors were drawn to Tunisia for its sunny climate and its bargain holidays in one of the amazing beach resorts. It is true, the white sandy beaches are glorious, the sea often clear turquoise, and some of the resorts are among the best of what the Mediterranean has to offer. But this small country has so much more, mostly within easy reach of the coast: friendly people, well-preserved whitewashed *médinas*, green forests in the north, a vast desert and lush oases in the south, an amazing wealth of archaeological treasures inland and, last but not least, an exciting and delicious cuisine based on fresh local produce.

Inset: A *jetskier at Zarzis beach*
Below: *Visitors take to the 'ship of the desert'*

THE 10 ESSENTIALS

If you only have a short time to visit Tunisia, be sure not to leave the country without having sampled some of the essentials:

• **Buy a piece of pottery** such as an ashtray or vase, large plates or bowls. Blue and white are the traditional colours while fish decorations add extra value. Nabeul (➤ 52) and Guellala (➤ 79) are the major centres but pottery is on sale almost everywhere.

• **Eat a *brik*.** This unusual egg dish is popular as a starter at lunch or dinner, but take care, it is not the easiest thing to handle!

• **Head inland** to see the real Tunisia, with its magnificent countryside and spectacular Roman ruins.

• **Go to sleep** with a sweet-smelling sprig of jasmine on your pillow. Women wear garlands of the flower around their necks while men sometimes tuck one behind their ear.

• **Take a close look** at a traditional Tunisian door. Usually brightly painted, they are made of solid wood and decorated with black metal studs. You'll find these if you walk off the main drag of the *médina* in Tunis and get lost in its alleyways.

• **Ride a camel** at sunset in Douz (➤ 83), the gateway to the Sahara Desert.

• **Eat *baklava*,** a honey-laced pastry filled with crushed nuts, at one of the many *pâtisseries*.

• **Listen to the *muezzin*** calling the Muslim faithful to prayer five times a day. Many mosques are closed to non-Muslims but outside prayer hours you may be able to approach as far as the door for a glimpse.

• **Sleep in an underground cave** in the bizarrre landscape of Matmata (➤ 84), the set of a *Star Wars* movie.

• **Take home fresh dates**, extra virgin olive oil and a jar of fiery hot *harissa* paste.

Fish are a favourite motif for use in decorative work

The Shaping of Tunisia

Dido, Queen of Carthage, inspects the progress of work during the rebuilding of her city

c2000 BC
Berbers settle in Tunisia interbreeding with black Africans from south of the Sahara and blue-eyed, blond-haired immigrants from the north.

1100 BC
Phoenician traders establish trading posts along Tunisia's Mediterranean coastline including Sousse, Bizerte and Utica.

814 BC
The Phoenicians build the walled city of Carthage and rule a vast commercial empire for the next seven centuries.

146 BC
A long and violent struggle ends with the destruction of Carthage by the Romans.

44 BC
After defeating Pompey at the battle of Thapsus near Mahdia, Julius Caesar rebuilds Carthage. Over the next 400 years it becomes a major administrative centre and the third largest city of the Roman Empire.

AD 423
Carthage is destroyed by the Vandals, a Germanic tribe which has already pillaged its way through France and Spain, desecrating religious images.

533
Byzantines restore the port of Carthage and create a series of massive fortresses and magnificent churches.

647
Following the death of the Prophet Mohammed in 632, Arab armies arrive from the east killing the Byzantine Prefect Gregory at Sbeïtia in 647 and imposing Islam on the population.

797
Ibrahim ibn al Aghlab puts down a revolt and founds a dynasty. The Aghlabids build the Grande Mosquée de Sidi Oqba at Kairouan and the Grande Mosquée at Sousse, and introduce a sophisticated irrigation system, planting thousands of citrus trees.

909–1229
The Fatmids, Zirids, Almohads and Almoravids take turns at control.

1230–1574
The Hafsids make Tunis the capital and establish international trade in

gold, ostrich feathers, ebony, ivory and precious oils during a relatively long period of stability. This is followed by a century of decline.

1574
After a power struggle between the Ottoman Turks and Spanish Hapsburgs Tunis comes under the control of the Ottoman Empire, which appoints a ruling *pasha* who relies on a network of local *beys* (provincial governors) to enforce laws and collect taxes.

1704–1881
Hussein ibn Ali Turki takes control. Under the Husaynids the economy prospers as the *beys* exercise their monopoly to generate a vibrant trade in agricultural products.

1878
The Ottoman Empire is divided up at the Congress of Berlin and France announces it has a claim on Tunisia. Later it invades the country and in 1883 declares Tunisia a French protectorate.

1934
Radical lawyer Habib Bourguiba (▶ 14) forms the Neo-Destour Party.

1938
Anti-French demonstrators are killed by troops in Tunis. Bourguiba is arrested and imprisoned in France.

1956
Tunisia gains independence from France and a year later declares itself a republic with Habib Bourguiba as its first president.

1987
President Bourguiba is removed from office by his prime minister, the former army general Zine el-Abidine Ben Ali.

1988
Tunisia forms the Union du Grand Maghreb (Arab Maghreb Union) with Morocco, Algeria, Libya and Mauritania to help counter the impact of the European Union.

1991
President Ben Ali condemns the Iraqi invasion of Kuwait, but does not send troops to join the US-led Desert Shield force against Iraq.

1995
Tunisia signs an association agreement with the European Union which will lead to free trade with the EU after 12 years.

2000
Habib Bourguiba dies.

Habib Bourguiba, depicted with his dog, is commemorated by this statue in the public gardens in central Tabarka

Peace & Quiet

It is easy to get away from it all in Tunisia, since there is only one major city and much of the rest of the country is sparsely populated. The country has only a handful of national parks and municipal gardens, but there are few restrictions on wandering in the countryside.

The Coastline

The Roman historian Pliny the Elder (AD 23–79) described the Tunisian coastline as being one of the finest in the world, and nearly 2,000 years later he would probably still hold the same view. Tourist resorts have developed along some of the finest stretches of beach, but with more than 1,100km of coastline available, much of the rest remains completely unspoilt.

Quieter beaches include Raf Raf Plage, a glorious crescent-shaped stretch of fine white sand 38km east of Bizerte facing the small rocky island of Pilau, which is good for snorkelling and underwater fishing. The beach is partly bordered by the small village of Raf Raf and by dunes and pinewoods. Near by is the isolated beach of Sidi Ali el Mekki, where a small number of cafés and a few straw huts for camping are the only facilities. To the west of Bizerte, Rass Engelah is overlooked by a picturesque Moorish lighthouse.

The area around Tabarka has been dubbed the 'Coral Coast' (▶ 43) and the waters are so crystal clear that it offers excellent diving.

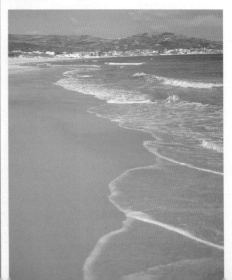

The beach at Raf Raf is popular with day trippers from Bizerte and Tunis

The Desert

The Sahara Desert covers nearly the whole of southern Tunisia and the popular image of shifting sands sweeping across a relentlessly barren landscape is an accurate description of the landscape found in the Grand Erg Oriental. Only suitable for four-wheel-drive vehicles and then only when accompanied by skilled drivers and guides, most holidaymakers are content to experience a less harsh version of the desert.

This can be found in the area around Tunisia's two great *chotts* (salt lakes), Chott el Jerid (► 82) and Chott el Gharsa (► 87), which sit below sea level and are fringed

Wind-furrowed sand dunes near Douz

by beautiful oases. Only a few kilometres outside the main desert centres of Nefta (► 85) and Tozeur (► 87) one can be driving on a totally empty road. Get out and walk around and the silence is almost deafening. Douz (► 83) is one of the best places to go for a camel ride into the desert.

DID YOU KNOW?

Arabs have more than a hundred different words to describe a camel. A familiar sight in the southern half of the country, the so-called 'ship of the desert' is an extraordinary animal which can survive for months without water and when it does finally get the chance for a drink it can consume up to 130 litres in one go. Talk about quenching your thirst!

Flora and Fauna

Tunisia was once home to an exotic array of wildlife, including lions and elephants, which has long since disappeared. Today the largest animal existing in any number is

Prickly pears are known here as Barbary figs

the wild boar which is found in the forests around Tabarka (► 43) where there are also jackals, porcupines and mongooses. Wild animals in the desert region include foxes, snakes, horned vipers and scorpions – so it is best not to walk around barefoot!

More than two hundred different species of bird have been recorded in Tunisia. Jebel Ichkeul National Park (► 19, Top Ten) is a stopping-off point in the spring and autumn migration seasons between Europe and Africa.

Tunisia's Famous

Below: *Habib Bourguiba strove for independence from French rule, and instituted education for all*

Habib Bourguiba (1903–2000)

Habib Bourguiba became the republic's first president and is widely known as the father of modern Tunisia. He was born in Monastir in 1903 and educated at the elite Sadiki College in Tunis, and in Paris where he studied law. Bourguiba's political career did not begin until 1932 when, back in Tunis, he started a newspaper, *L'Action Tunisienne*. Two years later he founded the populist Neo-Destour Party which was committed to independence from France. Six months after its foundation the party was declared illegal and for the first of many times over the next two decades Bourguiba was arrested and imprisoned.

Immediately after World War II Bourguiba travelled to many world capitals highlighting Tunisia's plight, gaining considerable support. In 1955 he accepted a French plan for an autonomous state and on 20 March 1956 the country gained independence. The following year the new republic was established and Bourguiba became its first president. He governed for 31 years, until removed from office by the current president Zine el-Abidine Ben Ali. He was sometimes criticised for his autocratic style but his achievements included forging a strong national identity, providing for universal education and elevating the role of women in Tunisian society.

Ibn Khaldun (1332–1406)
Ibn Khaldun, the Tunis-born philosopher and politician, spent four years writing a massive volume on North African history but made a greater impact with *Muqaddima*, a brief introduction to the history of the world. Khaldun is thought to be the first person to write about cyclical patterns in history and the nature and development of society, which now form some of the basic principles of modern-day sociology.

Hannibal (247–182 BC)

Hannibal, although born in Spain, is considered an honorary Tunisian as his birth took place on Carthaginian territory. His most famous exploit occurred during the second Punic war when he invaded Italy from the north after crossing the Alps with an army of 40,000 men and 300 elephants.

Support from Carthage collapsed just as Rome seemed to be within his grasp and he was recalled home. In 202 BC Hannibal was defeated by the Roman general Scipio Africanus at the battle of Zama near Le Kef. Forced into exile in Syria and later to (what is now) Turkey, he committed suicide by poison to avoid capture by the Romans.

Right: *after crossing the Alps with his elephants, Hannibal descends into Italy*

Top Ten

Above: *Parts of Ksar Ouled Soltane are over 400 years old*
Right: *Tunisia's most famous mosaic depicts Virgil, Clio and Melpomene*

15

1
Dougga

 28B5

 110km southwest of Tunis

🕐 Daily 8–7 (8.30–5.30 in winter)

🍴 Restaurant Mercure (£–££) near the ticket office, Nouvelle Dougga (closed Mon in winter; small café (£) near main entrance

🚌 Hourly daytime services from Tunis to Le Kef which stop at Nouvelle Dougga 3km from the site. Difficult to reach the site without a car. Taxis available from Téboursouk

✋ Cheap

❓ Summer plays and concerts in Dougga's theatre. Times and dates variable

Dougga is a splendid monument to Roman precision building

Tunisia's best–preserved and most spectacular Roman ruins have a dramatic setting on a hillside with wide views of the surrounding countryside.

The Roman town of Dougga, a UNESCO World Heritage Site, was built on the ancient settlement of Thugga, which had become the seat of the Numidian king Massinissa in the 2nd century BC. Dougga prospered under Roman rule and at its peak is thought to have had a population of 10,000 people. In the early 1950s residents were moved to the nearby purpose-built village of Nouvelle Dougga.

Fervent archaeologists will find Dougga worth a full day's visit, and even those with a limited interest need to allow at least two hours just to see the main buildings. It is advisable – particularly in summer – to arrive as early as possible to avoid the crowds and intense midday heat.

The heavily restored Roman Theatre, cut into the hillside, is the most complete of any in Tunisia and is still used for the Dougga festival in the summer. There is a magnificent view over the surrounding wheat fields and olive groves from the impressive Temple of Saturn, dedicated to the sun god Baal Hammon. The centrepiece of the nearby Plaza of the Winds is a compass-like wind-indicator inscribed with the names of the 12 Roman winds. Dougga's star attraction is the well-preserved Capitol built in AD 166 and dedicated to Jupiter, Juno and Minerva. Near the Arch of Severus is the attractive temple of Caelestis with a beautiful semi-circular portico. The house of Trifolium is thought to have been the brothel; the latrines immediately beside it have been very well preserved.

2
El Jem

The amphitheatre at El Jem is one of the Roman Empire's greatest legacies to Tunisia.

El Jem is only slightly smaller than the Colosseum in Rome, but it is better preserved and much more imposing, though situated incongruously at the end of a street of modern houses. If it were near a major European holiday destination there is little doubt it would be packed solid with visitors year-round, so try to see it soon before the crowds get there. Early morning is good for taking photographs and dusk is particularly atmospheric.

Pleasingly, there are very few signs inside the amphitheatre, making it easier to imagine the colourful festivals or the bloody dawn-to-dusk gladiatorial contests that were held here. The gladiators – often simply petty thieves, debtors or prisoners – would be pitted against each other or against wild animals to fight to the death.

Built between AD 230 and 238 in the busy market town of Thysdrus, the amphitheatre could seat crowds of more than 30,000. Measuring 149m long by 124m wide, even today it would be considered an impressive building achievement but without modern equipment it is an awesome feat of engineering. In the absence of suitable materials locally, blocks of sandstone were transported from quarries 30km away while water was carried 15km through an underground aqueduct.

El Jem archaeological museum has attractive 3rd-century mosaics. Behind the museum is Maison d'Africa, a complete and stunning Roman villa with a garden and a pool.

✚ 28C5

✉ 70km south of Sousse

🕐 Daily 7–7 (8–6 in winter)

🍴 Cafés (£) directly opposite entrance to the amphitheatre

🚌 On the main line south to Gafsa and Gabès and north to Sousse and Tunis

♿ None

✋ Moderate

❓ International Festival of Symphonic Music in July

Archaeological Museum

✉ 1km south of the amphitheatre on the road to Sfax

🕐 7–7 (8–5.30 in winter)

✋ Included in price of ticket to amphitheatre

The Roman amphitheatre at El Jem could hold 30,000

3
Iles Kerkennah

A watchtower built in the 16th century for surveying the islands

The cluster of seven islands 20km off the coast of Sfax has been called 'The Last Paradise' and would appeal to anyone trying to get away from it all.

 28C4

www.kerkennah.com

 20km east of Sfax

 La Sirène (££) on the beachfront in Remla (► 96)

Regular ferry services from Sfax to Sidi Youssef. The journey takes about an hour with at least four services a day in winter and departures every two hours in summer

Buses meet all ferries and all stop in Remla and al-Attaia

None

Once a place of exile for the Carthaginian general Hannibal and Tunisia's former president Habib Bourguiba (► 14), there are two main inhabited islands, Chergui and Gharbi, joined together by a causeway. The islands are reached by ferry from Sfax, arriving at Sidi Youssef on the south-western tip of the islands, with a single main road running 35km north to the fishing village of El Attaia.

Fishing remains the main source of income for most of the 15,000 islanders. Strings of clay pots for catching squid can be seen on many quaysides; palm fronds are used to channel fish into waiting nets. Although tourism now supplements the islands' economy it remains very low-key and recent plans by the Tunisian government to transform Iles Kerkennah into a massive purpose-built resort area appear to have been dropped. The small west coast tourist zone of Sidi Frej consists of a handful of modest hotels.

Borj el-Hissar, a ruined Aghlabid fort 3km north of Sidi Frej, was rebuilt by the Spanish in the 16th century; it is surrounded by Roman ruins and has the remains of several mosaics. Remla, the biggest settlement, has a few shops and cafés and one hotel, the Jazira (► 104). With its shallow waters and long stretches of empty sandy beaches, the area is well-suited to walking and cycling.

4
Jebel Ichkeul
National Park

One of only two wetland conservation areas to be designated World Heritage Sites by UNESCO (the other is the Everglades in Florida).

Telescopes enable visitors to view the birdlife of Lake Ichkeul

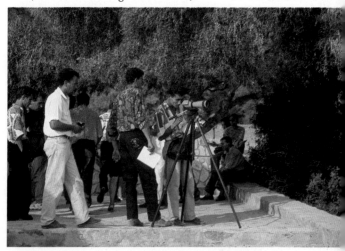

Jebel Ichkeul is the most important bird sanctuary in North Africa and provides a vital stopping point for birds migrating between Europe and Africa. If you visit at dawn or dusk from October to February, thousands of waterfowl can be spotted on the lake.

Rarer birds on the lake include the marbled teal and the purple gallinule, one of Tunisia's most colourful birds. Looking rather like an oversized moorhen, it has a bright red beak and gleaming purple-blue plumage. Sandpipers, stints and stilts are regularly found on the shores of Lac d'Ichkeul and Moussier's redstarts which are indigenous to North Africa can be spotted in the scrub. The park is also home to many animals including water buffalo, wild boar, jackals, otters and porcupines.

The park is a tranquil and uplifting place to visit at any time of the year; there are some picnic tables and several walking trails. Poppies and wild chrysanthemums bloom in the fields around the lake, and from the car park a steep climb leads to a small **Eco-Museum** which details the area's flora and fauna and explains the ecological importance of the lake. It also has a collection of stuffed birds.

There is nowhere to stay in the park and camping is not permitted, but it makes an easy day trip from Tunis.

28B6

30km southwest of Bizerte

Daily 6–8 (8–6 in winter)

Bring your own picnic, tables provided

No public transport; hire car essential, or bus to Menzel Bouguiba and then taxi

None

Free

Eco-Museum

9–12, 1.30–4.30

None

Free

5
Kairouan

 28B5

✉ 70km west of Sousse

🍴 Sabra (£), avenue de la
République – good
value set menus.
Sofra (££) at Hotel
RaKasbah on avenue
Ibn el-Jazzar

🚌 Bus station on the main
route between Tunis
and the south

ℹ️ Place des Martyrs
☎ 77 231897
🕐 Summer: Mon–Sat
8–7, Sun 8–noon;
winter: Mon–Thu 9–1,
3–6, Fri–Sat 8.30–1.
Multiple entry ticket
provides access to most
of the city's major
attractions, available at
the APPC at the
Aghlabid pools

**Grande Mosquée de Sidi
Oqba**

✉ Entrance on rue Ibrahim
ibn el-Aghlab

🕐 Sun–Thu 8.30–2, Fri
8.30–noon

  Entry on multiple ticket
(moderate)

 None

*Kairouan is Tunisia's holiest city, with more than
50 mosques within the médina.*

Kairouan is the fourth most important city in the Islamic
world after Mecca, Medina and Jerusalem. The **Grande
Mosquée de Sidi Oqba** (Great Mosque) is the star
attraction here; the existing building was constructed by
the Aghlabids in AD 863. Non-Muslims are forbidden to
enter the prayer hall with its 400 marble pillars, many of
which were recovered from the ruins of Carthage and El
Jem, but visitors may be allowed to take a look through
one of the 17 heavy cedar wood doors at one of the
world's oldest pulpits decorated with 250 carved wood
panels. Entry may also be permitted to the 128-step
staircase – made from Christian tombstones – to the top of
the square minaret for a superb panorama of the city.

The Mosquée des Trois Portes (Mosque of the Three
Doors) also dates from the 9th century and features three
arched doorways providing separate entrances for men,
women and children.

The Zaouia de Sidi Sahab (Shrine of the Companion) on
avenue de la République is the burial place of Abou Zamaa
el-Balaoui, a friend of the Prophet. It is sometimes known
as the Barber's Mosque as el-Balaoui always wore a
medallion containing three hairs from the Prophet's beard.
The original mausoleum dates back to the 7th century but
tiled archways, antechambers and beautiful floral mosaics
were added at the end of the 17th century.

The Bassins des Aglabides (Aghlabid Pools), ten
minutes' walk to the east, were part of an elaborate 9th
century water system which collected rain from the Tell
Plateau via a 35km aqueduct.

*Footwear is removed
before entering the prayer
hall of the Zaouia de Sidi
Sahab*

6
Ksar Ouled Soltane

➕ 28C3

✉ 22km east of Tataouine

🕐 All day

🍴 Hôtel les Ghorfas (£),
6km west of Metameur;
Hôtel Ksar Hadada (£)

🚌 Three buses a day from
Tataouine

✋ Free

❓ Ksar Hallouf (☎ 75
637148). Ruins of 12th-
century *ksar* 8km west

*The exterior steps of the
ksour look less than safe*

*One of the enduring legacies of the Berber culture,
ksour originally served as fortified grain stores
(and some still do).*

Built from mud and stone, ksour (singular 'ksar') are a familiar sight in southern Tunisia especially around Tataouine. In the hostile desert climate there might only be a good crop once every few years making it essential to defend supplies from attack by other tribes. Cool conditions inside the ksour's claustrophobic, barrel-vaulted rooms (known as ghorfas) meant that grain could be kept for several years without deteriorating. It was typical for ksour to be clustered together around a courtyard and to be linked by internal steps and passageways. Usually three or four stories high, some of the ksour in this region have precarious-looking outside steps.

The earliest surviving *ksour* are up to 800 years old but Ksar Ouled Soltane is among the best-known because it is particularly well preserved. Buildings in the first courtyard are more than 400 years old while the second complex dates from around 1850. Off the beaten track, it is rarely visited and remains a storage place for the grain and olives of the Ouled Chehida who built it. One of the most rewarding times to visit is on Friday afternoons, when the courtyard becomes a meeting point for the local community.

A visit to Ouled Soltane is often combined with trips to other *ksour* in the area including the 13th-century Ksar Hallouf near Zammour, part of which has been converted into a very simple hotel with primitive toilet facilities. Better quality accommodation and lunches are available at the *600-year-old ksar* in Metameur, 6km west of Medenine.

7
Musée du Bardo, Tunis

Tunisia's national museum houses archaeological treasures from all over the country but the highlight is its impressive collection of mosaics.

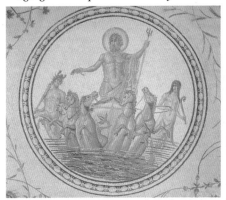

✚ 32A2 (arrowed)

✉ Route de Bizerte, Quartier Le Bardo, 6km from city centre

☎ 71 513842

🕐 Tue–Sun 9–5; 9.30–4.30 in winter. Closed Mon

🍽 Small café on ground floor (£)

🚇 Line 4 from Tunis city centre

🚌 3 from avenue Habib Bourguiba

♿ Few

✋ Moderate

The Musée du Bardo is housed in a grand former palace of the Husaynid *beys* (provincial governors). It is arranged in sections covering the Carthaginian, Roman, early Christian and Islamic eras. The first rooms are dedicated to the Punic period with stelae, masks and a priceless terracotta statue of the sun god, Baal Hammon sitting on a throne, wearing a feathered head-dress. The Roman section, where entire walls and floors are paved with mosaics from the 2nd century BC to the 7th century AD, many almost intact. The 3rd-century mosaic of the poet Virgil writing the *Aeneid* attended by two muses, found in a villa in Sousse (▶ 60), and the giant Triumph of Neptune mosaic are among the most exceptional exhibits. Another captivating 3rd-century work which was found at Dougga (▶ 16, Top Ten) is the mosaic of Ulysses and his sailors resisting the songs of three sirens trying to lure their vessel on to the rocks. The mosaic of Perseus rescuing Andromeda from the clutches of a sea monster was taken from an underground villa at Bulla Regia (▶ 42). Many of the smaller mosaics feature common themes including hunting and farming scenes, Greek and Roman gods, the sea, battles and family life. Animals, birds and fish are also widely depicted. There is also a spectacular collection of Greek bronze and marble figures, which were recovered from a Greek shipwreck which occurred off the coast of Mahdia in the first century BC.

Above left: *The* Triumph of Neptune *mosaic*
Above: *The magnificent decorated doorway to the Musée du Bardo*

8
Qasr el-Aïn, Nefta

➕ 28A4

✉ Avenue des Sources

🕐 All day

🍴 Café in the Corbeille (£);
Les Sources (££) on
avenue Bourguiba near
tourist office;
Bar La Corbeille (£)
overlooking the
Corbeille

🚌 Daily buses to Tunis,
Tozeur, Gafsa and
Kairouan from the bus
station on avenue Habib
Bourguiba

✈ Tozeur Airport 23km

✋ Free

ℹ Avenue Habib
Bourguiba ☎ 76
457236 🕐 Daily
8.30–noon, 2.40–7 (6 in
winter)

*Bunches of ripening fruit
hang from a date palm in
the Corbeille*

*Nefta is the most important religious centre in
Tunisia after Kairouan. The palms of the Corbeille
appear as a mirage coming from the desert.*

Legend has it that Nefta was first settled by Kostel, Noah's
grandson, as it was the place where water boiled for the
first time after the Flood. The oasis has a long tradition of
Sufism, a mystical 'branch' of Islam. The small oasis has
more than 20 mosques and more than a hundred shrines,
the tombs of *marabout* or local holy men, are scattered
among the palm trees. Many mosques and shrines (most
are closed to non-Muslims) suffered severe damage after
the torrential rains and floods in 1990, but most have been
restored. The Zaouia of Sidi Brahim is a complex of tombs
and a *medresa* of the Qadria, the most important Sufi
brotherhood. The Tomb of Marabout Sidi bou Ali is also
popular, as this holy man, born in Morocco but venerated
in Tunisia, is believed to have planted the first date seeds
in the oasis.

Nefta was known as the Princess of the Desert until
recently because of its Corbeille, a massive crater filled
with hundreds of palm trees and dotted with white
shrines. It was fed by 152 natural springs, many of them
warm and sulphurous, but unfortunatley these have dried
up and water is now pumped in from a large pool at the
west of the oasis. The best views, although these days the
groves are pooly kept, are from the hotels Bel Horizon and
Sahara Palace.

Nefta's main oasis, now watered by the same pool, has
hundreds of palms, yielding excellent dates.

9
Sidi Bou Saïd

Sidi Bou Saïd is like a big balcony overlooking the sea. For centuries this tiny white-and-blue village has attracted writers and artists.

The village's history goes back, however, to the ninth century when a *ribat* (fortified monastery) was built against the Christian invaders. In the 13th century a community settled around the tomb of the holy man, Sidi bou Said, whose life is still celebrated during a festival in August. Europeans were not allowed into the village until 1820, but the flow since then has not stopped, including Gustave Flaubert who wrote *Salambo* here, Paul Klee, Simone de Beauvoir, André Gide and Michel Foucault.

Many artists still live here and though Sidi Bou, as it is affectionately called, now also attracts masses of tourists – particularly in summer – it has kept its peculiar charm. The French baron Rodolphe d'Erlanger fell in love with the village at 16 and built a sumptuous cliffside home here, while other wealthy French visitors restored houses. In 1915 d'Erlanger obtained a declaration from the Bey of Tunis to keep and protect the whitewashed architecture of the village, and to paint all the woodwork in the typical blue. D'Erlanger's villa, the Dar Ennejma Ezzahra, has now become a centre for Arab and Mediterranean music, with a beautiful collection of musical instruments and an interesting archive.

The cobbled street goes up to the main square with the atmospheric Café des Nattes. On the way is Dar al Annabi, partly residential and partly forklore museum. Stroll through the side steets to Café Sidi Chabanne on the bay.

✚ 28B6

✉ 20km northeast of Tunis.

🍴 Mint tea and coffee at Café des Nattes (£) and Café Sidi Chabanne (£) (► 92)

🚉 TGM metro services from Tunis every 20 mins. Journey time 30 mins. 15 min uphill walk from the station to the centre of the village

♿ None

❓ Celebration of the life of Sidi Bou Saïd in August

Le Centre des Musiques Arabes et Mediterranéennes

✉ Ennejma Ezzahra

🕐 Tue–Sun, 8.30–1, 3–6 (9–1, 2–5 only in winter). Closed Mon

✋ Inexpensive

Blue doors, flowers and dazzling white walls in Sidi Bou Saïd

10
Thermes d'Antonin
(Antonine Baths)

Once the biggest Roman baths in the Empire and Carthage's best-preserved site.

 37C2

 Avenue des Thermes d'Antonin

Daily 8–7 (8.30–5.30 in winter). Closed on public holidays

Drinks at Café des Nattes or Café Sidi Chabanne, Sidi Bou Saïd (▶92)

Regular TGM metro services from Tunis to Carthage–Hannibal station

None

Moderate (ticket will also provide entry to other Carthage ruins and the Musée National de Carthage)

The site is entered from the top of a colourful garden which slopes gently down to the sea following the pattern of the original Roman streets. Close to the entrance are the remains of a *schola* which was a kind of after-school boys' club for the sons of wealthy Romans, with an unusual mosaic showing children doing physical exercises. The ruins of the Byzantine Basilica of Douimes are marked by three rows of double pillars and a mosaic floor.

Visitors are not allowed to enter the baths, but can study them from a viewing platform. A white marble model shows what the baths would have been like when they were in daily use and a couple of pillars have been repositioned to give an idea of the original height.

Work on the baths began during the reign of the Roman Emperor Hadrian (AD 76–138) who spent a considerable amount of time touring his vast empire and promoting urban life. It is hard to imagine the grandeur, but to get an idea: when the public toilets were discovered, they were at first thought to be a theatre. Heat was provided by an underground system of furnaces and there was a series of hot rooms of varying temperatures, a cold plunge pool and a Roman 'whirlpool', (without the bubbles of course).

The baths are surrounded by an archaeological park with a number of Punic tombs, and the site borders the presidential palace, the official residence of the Tunisian leader, President Ben Ali.

Above: *A section of the great bathhouse complex*

What to See

Above: *Scarlet national flags of Tunisia outside the Palais du Congrès*
Right: *An Arab horseman at the Festival of the Sahara, Douz*

TUNISIA

La Galite

Cap Blanc
Bizerte Utica
Parc National Tinja Ghar el Melh
de Jebel Ichkeul
Sidi Mechrig **Mateur** Menzel Gammarth Cap Bon
Bourguiba La Marsa El Haouaria
Tabarka Béja **Mejez** Sidi Bou Saïd Kerkouane
Aïn Draham **El Bab** Korbous **Kelibia**
Thuburnica Bou Salem **TUNIS** Carthage
Bulla Regia La Goulette **Menze Temime**
Jendouba Testour Korba
Teboursouk **Zaghouan** **Nabeul**
Dougga Thuburbo **Hammamet**
Le Kef Majus **El Fahs**
Enfida
Makthar Hergla
Kairouan Port el Kantaoui
Thala Skanès
Sousse
Monastir
T e l l Moknine
Ruines
de Sbeitla **Mahdia**
Kasserine Ksour Essaf
El Jem
1544 m **Sbeitla**
Jebel Rass
Chambi Kaboudia
Sidi Bouzid
Sfax
Midès Meknassy Iles
Tamerza Gorges **Gafsa** Kerkennah
de Selja Mahrès
Chebika El Guettar
Metlaoui *Golfe de*
Chott *Gabès* **Houmt-**
el Gharsa Degache **Souk**
Nefta Tozeur **Gabès** Midoun
Erriadh *Ile de Jerba*
Qasr el-Aïn Ajim El Kantara
Chott el Jerid Kebili Guellala
Matmata Metameur **Zarzis**
Douz **Medenine**
Ksar Hallouf
Ksar Haddada Foum Ben
Ghomrassen Tataouine Gardane
Ksar Ghilane Chenini
Ksar Ouled
Soltane
Grand Erg
Oriental
Remada
Dehibat

DZ

L-R

Borj el Khadra

0 50 100 150 km

A B C

Tunis & the North

Although northern Tunisia is home to nearly a quarter of the population, thousands of holidaymakers bypass this area altogether and head straight for the east coast beach resorts. This is a pity as the capital is here and the surrounding countryside and coastline are enormously varied.

Tunis has more than enough attractions to warrant a few nights' stay or, at the very least, a full day's excursion. For more than 3,000 years, Tunis has been among the great cities of the Mediterranean and it still has plenty to offer. It would also provide a convenient base for independent travellers, with dozens of quiet beaches and some of the country's finest archaeological sites within easy reach.

Tabarka is emerging as Tunisia's northern flagship resort, while the charming old port town of Bizerte is still debating whether it really wants to entice international tourists or is quite content to remain a sleepy backwater.

> *'Around Carthage, immobile waves glistened as the moon spread its beams on the gulf surrounded by mountains and on the Lake of Tunis.'*
>
> GUSTAVE FLAUBERT,
> 1821–80

Tunis

Tunis started life as a small garrison town, defended by the high walls of its *médina*. Its expansion into a wealthy trading city was sparked by the Arab invasion of Tunisia in the 7th century, though it was another 600 years before Tunis became the capital.

28B6
66km southeast of Bizerte, 120km northwest of Sousse
1 avenue Mohamed V
71 341077
Mon–Sat 8–6, Sun 9–noon

Today the city is the undisputed focal point of the nation. It is home to one in ten of the population and forms the epicentre of political, cultural and social life. The city combines a vibrant, atmospheric old town of narrow lanes and covered *souqs* with the more European-style Ville Nouvelle characterised by tree-lined avenues and elegant colonnaded, balconied buildings.

What to See in Tunis

33C2
Café at Hotel Africa (£) (➤ 101), 50 avenue Habib Bourguiba; Chez Nous (££–£££) (➤ 93)
5, 8, 35, 50
Line 1, Tunis Marine

Cathédrale de St Vincente de Paul
33C2
Avenue Habib Bourguiba
Daily service at 6.30am and Sundays at 9 and 11am
Free (donations accepted)

Above: The Avenue imparts something of a French air to the city

AVENUE HABIB BOURGUIBA ✪

The 'Champs Elysées' of Tunis, avenue Habib Bourguiba is the capital's best-known and most prestigious thoroughfare, where seemingly the whole city comes for a late afternoon coffee. Apart from a few grand buildings there is a mishmash of banks, *bureaux de change*, *pâtisseries*, cinemas, car rental agents and hotels, including Hotel Africa – the most prominent landmark and a popular meeting place (➤ 101).

Avenue Habib Bourguiba begins at the foot of avenue de France close to the main entrance to the *médina*. Where the streets run together is the **Cathédrale de St Vincente de Paul**, a Catholic church built in 1882. Just across the road is the Ambassade de France (French Embassy) from where the Protectorate was governed between 1881 and the granting of independence in 1956. Further east is the art nouveau-style old French Théâtre Municipal which regularly features good Arabic and classical music concerts.

JEMAA EZ ZITOUNA ✪✪

Jemaa ez Zitouna (the Great Mosque) covers an area of more than 5,000 sq m and is the largest mosque in Tunis, dwarfing the surrounding alleyways. It has been at the spiritual heart of Tunis for over 1,000 years and is the only mosque in the city which can be visited by non-Muslims, though access is restricted to a viewing enclosure overlooking the polished marble courtyard.

Jemaa ez Zitouna (literally Mosque of the Olive Tree) dates mostly from the middle of the 9th century, though it has been modified many times since, and was inspired by the slightly larger Grande Mosquée de Sidi Oqba (Great Mosque) in Kairouan (► 20, Top Ten). Its outer wall is built of stone taken from Roman Carthage. The courtyard is flanked on three sides by simple arcades and on the fourth by a prayer hall supported by 184 columns.

During the 13th and 14th centuries the mosque became an important Islamic university attracting students from all over the Arab world. It continued to flourish until the 1950s when the teaching faculty was closed on the orders of President Bourguiba in a bid to reduce religious influence in the country. The mosque and its 500-year-old library, containing one of the world's greatest collections of Arab literature, had its teaching status restored in 1987 by President Ben Ali.

✚	32B2
✉	Rue Jemaa ez Zitouna
⏰	8am–noon. Closed Fri
🍴	Café ez Zitouna (£), rue Jemaa ez Zitouna
🚌	1
🚇	Habib Thameur
♿	None
💷	Cheap

The square minaret of Jemaa ez Zitouna can be seen from rooftop terraces in the souq

TUNIS

5   Parc du Belvédère   PLACE PASTEU

Musée des Arts

EL OMRANE

LA MAISON

Jardin Zoologique

4

AVENUE OULED HAFFOUZ

AVENUE TAIEB MEHIRI

AVENUE HEDI

AVENUE MEHTAR SAADALLAH

BOULEVARD B. BEN CHAABANE

BOULEVARD HEDI SAÏD

AVENUE BECHIR SFAR

BAB SOUÏKA

AVE

AVE

BAB BOU
3 SAÄDOUN

RUE BAB BOU SAADOUN

BOULEVARD DE

RUE BAB BOU SAADOUN

AVE

Pa
Hab
Thame

BAB SOUÏKA

PLACE
BAB SOUÏKA

RUE MONG

Mosquée
Sidi Mahrez   MÉDINA

RUE ESSAFI

BOULEVARD BAB BENAT

Mosquée de
Hammoûda
Pacha
Dar
el Bey

Ambassade de
l'Angleterre
BAB EL BAHR

Musée
du Bardo

AVENUE DE LA RABTA

AVENUE DARGHOUTH PACHA

AVENUE ABDALLA IBN ABBES

AVENUE 9 AVRIL 1938

MÉLASSINE

Collège
Sadiki

Maison
du Parti
Kasbah

Mosquée
Sidi Youssef

Ste-Croix

Tombe
Jemaa ez Zitou
SOUQS Dar
Othma
Dar
Hussein

Marché
Ghal

Mosquée de
la Kasbah
Mosquée des
Teinturiers

BLVD BAB MENARA

Tourbet
el Bey

BAB EL JEDID   Musée des
Arts Populaires
et Traditions
(Dar Ben Abdalla

Parc
el Gorjani

MONTFLEUF

2

INTERCOMMUNALE SUD

BOULEVARD DU 9 AVR.

1

Sebkhet es-Sejoumi

0   ½   1 km

A   B   LA MANOUBIA

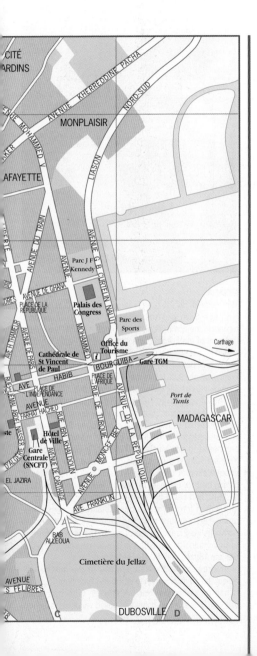

CITÉ
ARDINS

AVENUE KHERREDDINE PACHA

NORD-SUD

MONPLAISIR

AVENUE MOHAMMED V

AFAYETTE

LIASON

AVENUE DU TRAIN

AVENUE DE GHANA

AVENUE G. B. CURTELN NALU

AVENUE MOHAMMED

PLACE DE LA
RÉPUBLIQUE

Parc J F
Kennedy

Palais des
Congress

Parc des
Sports

Carthage

Office du
Tourisme
ℹ

Cathédrale de
St Vincent
de Paul

BOURGUIBA

Gare TGM

HABIB

PLACE DE
L'AFRIQUE

AVE

PLACE DE
L'INDÉPENDANCE

AVENUE

FARHAT HACHED

RUE IBN KHALDOUN

RUE DE TURQUIE

AVENUE DE

AVENUE DE LA RÉPUBLIQUE

Port de
Tunis

MADAGASCAR

ste

Hôtel
de Ville

Gare
Centrale
(SNCFT)

EL JAZIRA

AVENUE MONCEF BEY

AVENUE DE CARTHAGE

D'ALGER

AVE FRANKLIN

BAB
ALLEOUA

Cimetière du Jellaz

AVENUE
S FÉLIBRES

C

DUBOSVILLE   D

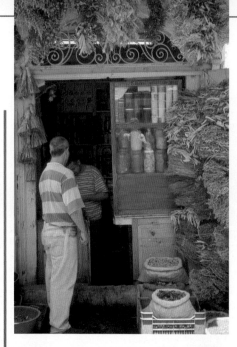

Right: *Sacks of spices and bundles of dried herbs give a particular scent to the* souq

Bab el Bahr
✚ 32B3
⊠ Place de la Victoire
🚌 1
🚇 Habib Thameur
🍴 Plenty of choice
♿ Difficult

Mosquée de Hammouda Pacha
✚ 32B2
⊠ Just off rue Sidi Ben Anous

Mosquée Sidi Youssef
✚ 32B2
⊠ Near Souk el-Berka

Dar Othman
✚ 32B2
⊠ rue el-M' Bazaa, off rue des Teinturiers
🕐 Not open to the public

Tourbet el Bey
✚ 32B2
⊠ rue Sidi Zamoul, off rue des Teinturiers
🕐 Mon–Sat 9.30–4.30
 Inexpensive

MÉDINA ●●●

The medieval part of Tunis is listed by UNESCO as a World Heritage Site. It dates back to the 7th century and remained the commercial centre of the city until the establishment of the French Protectorate in 1881, after which it began to decline. Start by exploring the narrow alleys at the **Bab el Bahr** (also known as the Sea Gate or Porte de France) on place de la Victoire. The arched gateway passes through the old city wall and dates from 1848.

The **Mosquée de Hammouda Pacha** with its thin Turkish-style minaret, built in 1655 to honour an Italian who had converted to Islam, and the **Mosquée Sidi Youssef** with an octagonal minaret, the oldest of its type in the city, are closed to non-Muslims. There is a good view of Sidi Youssef from the rooftop of the Musée des Turcs, an antique shop in the Souq et-Trouk. **Dar Othman** was a palace built for Othman Dey, who ruled Tunisia from 1598 to 1610, and has a pretty courtyard garden with cypress and lemon trees. The rue des Libraires contains three small 18th-century *medresa* (theological schools) at numbers 11, 27 and on the corner of the street. **Tourbet el Bey** in rue Tourbet el Bey is a royal mausoleum built in the late 18th century for the Husaynid princes.

A stroll around the northern part of the *médina* will reveal the small community which still lives here much as it has for centuries. Narrow streets, with traditional wooden, nail-studded doors and grilled windows, seem to keep their secrets to themselves.

MUSÉE DES ARTS POPULAIRES ET TRADITIONS

😊😊

The Museum of Popular Arts and Traditions occupies a late 18th-century palace, the Dar Ben Abdallah. The ornate entrance leads into a marble courtyard with a fountain, showing the visitor a tantalising example of the largely hidden side of the old city. In many ways the building itself is more interesting than the exhibition rooms which show upper class urban life in Tunis in the 19th century.

MUSÉE DU BARDO (► 23, TOP TEN)

PARC DU BELVÉDÈRE

😊

The Belvedere Park was laid out by the French as an exclusive enclave for the families of the ruling classes. Today, with so few green open spaces in the city, the park is a popular place to escape the summer heat. An elegant 18th-century pavilion (or *koubba*) is half-way up the hill and from the top there is a good view of the city. There is also a small zoo (► 110).

SOUQS

😊😊😊

Shopping in the *souqs* (markets) is one of the biggest attractions of the *médina* for many. The myriad tiny alleys provide endless opportunities for hunting down bargains and haggling. Originally each *souq* specialised in a single trade, although many now sell souvenirs. Among the oldest is the 13th-century Souq el Attarine (the perfume-makers' market) which still sells scents and essential oils. The Souq des Etoffes sells fabric and clothes; search out the Souq du Cuivre (coppersmiths), the Souq des Babouches (slippers), and the Souq el-Kebabjia (silk). The Souq et-Trouk (market of the Turks) was one of the city's finest when it opened in 1630, and the Souq el-Berka was one of the largest slave markets in the Mediterranean.

➕ 32B2
✉ Impasse Ben Abdallah, off rue Sidi Kacem
☎ 71 256195
🕐 Mon–Sat 9.30–4.30
🍴 Plenty of choice
🚌 1
Ⓖ Habib Thameur
♿ None
🎟 Inexpensive

➕ 32B5
✉ Avenue Taieb Mehiri
🕐 Open access but avoid at night
🍴 Couple of cafés serving drinks
🚌 5, 5c, 5d
Ⓖ Palestine
🎟 Free
❓ Concerts in summer

Zoo
🕐 9–7 (to 4 in winter)
🍴 Café
🎟 Cheap

Left: *Traditional Tunisian woollen hats on sale in the Souq des Chechias*

➕ 32B2
✉ Throughout the *médina*
🕐 Mostly closed on Sun
🍴 M'Rabet Café (£), Souq et-Trouk
🚌 1
Ⓖ Habib Thameur

The elegant façade of the National Museum

Carthage

Carthage is one of the best known of Tunisia's archaeological sites, though its impact is lessened by the way the surviving treasures are scattered over a large area in a suburb of the capital.

Founded in 814 BC by the Phoenicians, by the fourth century BC Carthage had become the centre of their vast maritime empire. In 146 BC it was destroyed by the Romans who – only 25 years later – began rebuilding on the same site. It became the third largest city of the Roman Empire before it was destroyed by the Arabs in AD 692, ending its heyday.

A complete tour will take all day; it is probably less overwhelming to make a couple of shorter trips. The Musée National de Carthage (▶ right) is worth a visit for an overview of the site and to see some of the magnificent treasures, dating back to the city's earliest days.

What to See in Carthage

BYRSA HILL ⭐⭐

It is possible to see the whole of the site from the summit of Byrsa Hill. This was the heart of the city under Punic rule and is the best place to start a tour. The **Cathédrale de St Louis** built here in 1890 is dedicated to the French king who died in 1279 while trying to lay siege to Tunis. The cathedral has been restored as a cultural centre for Arab music and is now known as the Acropolium.

CIMETIÈRE ⭐

The American War Cemetery commemorates the 6,564 Americans who died in North Africa during World War II. There are 2,840 neatly tended graves and a Wall of Remembrance naming those who were never found.

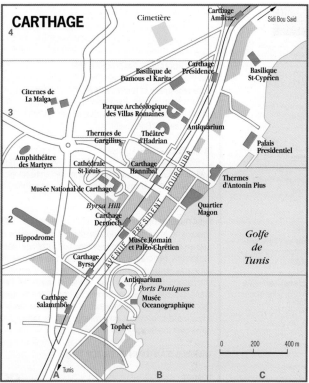

CARTHAGE

4 Cimetière Carthage Amilcar Sidi Bou Said

Basilique de Damous el Karita Carthage/Présidence Basilique St-Cyprien

Citernes de La Malga Parque Archéologique des Villas Romaines

3 Antiquarium

Thermes de Gargilius Théâtre d'Hadrian Palais Presidentiel

Amphithéâtre des Martyrs Cathédrale St-Louis Carthage Hannibal

Thermes d'Antonin Pius

Musée National de Carthage

Byrsa Hill Quartier Magon

2 Carthage Demech

Hippodrome Golfe de Tunis

Musée Romain et Paléo-Chrétien

Carthage Byrsa

Antiquarium

Ports Puniques

Carthage Salammbô Musée Oceanographique

1 Tophet

0 200 400 m

A B C

Tunis

LES PORTS PUNIQUES ✪

In the second century the twin Punic Ports provided berths for more than 200 naval ships but today it is almost impossible to imagine such a sight. The ports have shrunk to little more than ponds and the only way of making any sense of how they operated is to visit the small **Antiquarium** on the edge of the harbour to look at a scale model left behind by a British excavation team. It shows the ports as one giant shipyard surrounded by several slipways. The nearby **Musée Oceanographique** (Oceanographic Museum) has been modernised, with some interactive displays bringing a bit of life to an otherwise dull collection of fish and nauticalia.

✚ 37B1
✉ Rue Hannibal
🚉 Carthage–Salammbo

Antiquarium
✉ By the harbour
🕐 Opening times vary
💷 Free

Musée Oceanographique
✉ Avenue 2 Mars
☎ 71 730548
🕐 Tue–Sat 10–1, 3–6, Sun 10–6 💷 Cheap

MUSÉE NATIONAL DE CARTHAGE ✪✪✪

The National Museum of Carthage houses collections of sculpture, statues, masks and mosaics. On the ground floor are Carthaginian, Roman and Christian remains, while the first-floor has incense burners and plates found inside Punic graves as well as glass, ceramics and amphorae.

✚ 37B2
☎ 71 730036
✉ Near the cathedral
🕐 8–7 (8.30–5 in winter)
🚉 Demech or Hannibal
💷 Moderate

🔲 37B2
⏰ Daily 9–7 (9–5 in winter)
🚇 Carthage–Byrsa or Carthage–Dermech
💰 Cheap

🔲 37B2
✉ Avenue de la République
🚇 Carthage–Hannibal
♿ None

🔲 37B3
✉ Avenue 7 Novembre
🚇 Carthage–Hannibal
♿ None
💰 Cheap
❓ Carthage International Festival in the summer

🔲 37B1
✉ Avenue Farhat Hached
⏰ Daily 9–7 (9–5 in winter)
🚇 Carthage–Salammbo
♿ None
💰 Cheap

MUSÉE ROMAIN ET PALÉO-CHRÉTIEN ✪

The small Roman and Palaeo-Christian Museum is located at the crossroads of two ancient Roman streets over a still-intact Roman cistern. Excavations are still going on and exhibits include two peacock mosaics and a 5th-century marble statue of Ganymede.

QUARTIER MAGON ✪

Located close to the Thermes d'Antonin (▶ 26, Top Ten), the Magon Quarter has been turned into an archaeological park. There are two small exhibition rooms and a display of mosaic pavements.

THÉÂTRE D'HADRIAN ✪

There is little or nothing left of the original Theatre of Hadrian built in the early 2nd century, but it has now been completely restored and is very popular as a venue for concerts and plays during the annual Carthage International Festival. Just beyond the theatre is the Parc Archéologique des Villas Romaines (the Archaeological Park of Roman Villas), a collection of columns, statues and a few mosaics but most acknowledged for its setting with views over the Bay of Tunis.

THERMES D'ANTONIN (▶ 26, TOP TEN)

TOPHET ✪✪

It is hard to imagine this quiet, overgrown garden was used for child sacrifice. Excavations have unearthed more than 20,000 urns containing the ashes of boys aged between two and 12, sacrificed by Carthaginians in the 8th century BC. The remains were cremated as an offering to the sun god Baal Hammon and Tanit, the moon goddess.

Right: *Memorial stones at Tophet serve as reminders of a cruel ancient ritual*

What to See Around Tunis

GAMMARTH ⭐⭐

Once a quiet seaside village, Gammarth is now a wealthy suburb of greater Tunis, with several expensive hotels and good restaurants on the coast. In the 1950s the beaches were notorious for attracting European nudists and became known as the Baies des Singes (Bay of Monkeys). Raoued Plage, beyond Gammarth, is a fine stretch of sand and is packed with families during the summer.

Above the beaches, on the Hauts des Gammarth, is Jebel Khawi (Hollow Mountain), where there is a French military cemetery for more than 4,000 Frenchmen killed during World War II.

✚ 28B6
✉ 20km northeast of Tunis
🍴 Good choice (£–£££)
🚌 20b from Jardin Thameur in Tunis city centre
♿ Few

Above: *Climb Gammarth Heights for a view along the coast to Carthage*

LA GOULETTE ⭐⭐

Despite its rundown houses, crumbling *kasbah* and general air of neglect, La Goulette is very popular for its excellent fish restaurants attracting crowds from the city on summer weekends. Once a pirates' stronghold and home to a large Jewish community, La Goulette ('the gullet') is at the mouth of the Tunis canal and is still a major cargo and ferry port. The *kasbah*, built in 1535, was used as a dungeon for prisoners waiting to be taken to the *médina* in Tunis to be sold as slaves.

✚ 28B6
✉ 15km northeast of Tunis
🍴 Café Vert (£££) ✉ 68 avenue Franklin D. Roosevelt ☎ 71 736156
Ⓜ TGM from Tunis Marine
✈ Tunis–Carthage Airport 10km
♿ Few

LA MARSA ⭐⭐⭐

La Marsa is the most upmarket beachfront suburb on the Bay of Tunis. With a palm tree-lined corniche and a long sandy beach it is a popular beach destination on weekends for residents of Tunis, and a permanent home for the well-heeled. Two of the town's finest residences belong to the ambassadors of Britain and France.

✚ 28B6
✉ 15km northeast of Tunis
🍴 Several (££–£££) around the metro station
Ⓜ Regular TGM from Tunis
✈ Airport 12km
♿ Few

SIDI BOU SAÎD (▶ 25, TOP TEN)

The pretty French colonial church in the centre of Béja

What to See in the North

BÉJA ⭐

Once among the richest and most important towns of the Maghreb, Béja has lost much of its allure and influence. Formerly a Roman garrison, the town was destroyed by the Vandals in the fifth century and again in the tenth and 11th centuries. Since then it has become an important agricultural centre. The medina, although a bit run down, is very atmospheric with mosques, fountains and lively streets. However, locally handwoven blankets are sold in Souq en-Nehasach and rue el-Attarine is the food and spice market. The Byzantine *kasbah* is used by the military and is not open to the public. There are Colonial and Commonwealth war cemeteries out beyond the station.

BIZERTE ⭐⭐

Bizerte is the largest town on the north coast with a picturesque old port and bustling *médina*. It has only slowly begun to embrace tourism with the building of several hotels along the route de la Corniche but it is easily visited on a day trip from Tunis, less than an hour's drive away.

Bizerte has been a major port since the Phoenicians built a canal linking the inland Lac de Bizerte (Lake Bizerte) with the open sea, creating one of the finest harbours in the western Mediterranean. Known then as Hippo Zarytus, it was renamed Bizerte in 678 after being captured by the Arabs. In the 16th century – under Turkish rule – Bizerte became a pirates' den. The French made it their principal

---

**Béja sidebar:**

✚ 28B6
✉ 110km west of Tunis
🍴 Restaurant at Hotel Phénix, 8 avenue de la République ✉ 78 450188
🚍 Up to to seven trains a day to and from Tunis
🚌 Frequent services from Tunis
♿ Few

**Bizerte sidebar:**

✚ 28B6
✉ 66km northwest of Tunis
🍴 Le Bonheur (£), 31 rue Thaalbi (➤ 92). Le Sport Nautique (£££), boulevard Habib Bougatfa (➤ 92)
🚍 Station on rue de Russie
🚌 To Tunis every half-hour from Quai Tarik Ibn Zaid
ℹ In the old harbour ☎ 72 432897
♿ Few
❓ Bizerte Festival Jul/Aug

naval base in the late 19th century and it has remained a military centre with young men in uniform a common sight on the town's streets.

The Vieux Port (Old Port), surrounded by shops and cafés and dotted with colourful fishing boats, is the heart of the town. At the mouth of the harbour is the *kasbah*, which despite its Byzantine appearance dates mainly from the 17th century. In places the walls are up to 10m high and 11m thick, and within is a maze of narrow, winding passageways. Facing the *kasbah* is the smaller Sidi el-Hanni fortress, which has been turned into a small but dull **Musée Oceanographique** (Oceanographic Museum), featuring a motley collection of local fish.

West of the *kasbah* is the *médina*, which was heavily bombed during World War II. Closed to non-Muslims, the 17th-century Grande Mosquée (Great Mosque) with its octagonal minaret is best viewed from rue des Armuriers in the street behind or, better still, from the opposite side of the harbour. The **Zaouia de Sidi Mokhtar** houses the local branch of the Association de Sauvegarde de la Médina, which seeks to preserve and restore the area. Displays include a map of the town showing how it looked in 1881. North of the *médina* the **Fort d'Espagne** (Spanish Fort, which was actually built by the Turks in the 1570s) offers an excellent view over Bizerte. The main beach runs for 5km alongside the route de la Corniche to Cap Bizerte.

Kasbah
- ⊠ North of the Old Harbour
- 🕐 Tue–Sat 9–12.30, 3–7, Sun 9–7
- 💶 Cheap

Musée Oceanographique
- ⊠ Avenue Habib Bourguiba
- 🕐 Tue–Sat 9–12.30, 3–7, Sun 9–7
- 💶 Cheap

Zaouia de Sidi Mokhtar
- ⊠ Place Lahedine Bouchoucha
- 🕐 Exhibitions
- 💶 Free

Fort d'Espagne
- ⊠ Boulevard Hassan en Nouri
- 💶 Free

Colourful small fishing boats moored at the Old Port of Bizerte

➕ 28A6
✉ 60km south of Tabarka,
9km north of Jendouba
☎ 78 630554
⏰ Daily 8–7 (8.30–5.30 in
winter)
🍴 Nearest cafés and
restaurants at Jendouba
🚆 Four trains from
Jendouba to Tunis
🚌 To Jendouba from Tunis
or Bizerte (around 4
hours) and then taxi or
louage (shared taxi)
💰 Cheap

Above: *The monumental
ruins of the Memmian
Baths*
Opposite: *A good view
of Tabarka from the
Genoese fort across
the bay*

BULLA REGIA   ✪✪✪

This Roman site is as remarkable as Dougga but, because
it is off the beaten track, it is never overrun with visitors,
making it much more atmospheric. Neolithic tombs at the
site suggest Bulla Regia was inhabited long before the
Romans and it was certainly the capital of one of the short-
lived Numidian kingdoms. After it was annexed by
Emperor Hadrian in the 2nd century it became one of the
wealthiest Roman cities in North Africa.

The rich wheat and olive merchants of the town used to
escape the summer heat by retreating to underground
villas. Some of these were paved with beautiful mosaics
and though some of the best have been moved to the
Musée du Bardo in Tunis (▶ 23, Top Ten), others remain,
undisturbed for centuries. These include the mosaic of
Venus and a cupid riding on dolphins at the Maison
d'Amphitrite (House of Amphitrite); and a mosaic of
fishermen at the Maison de la Pêche (House of Fishing),
the oldest surviving villa. La Maison de la Chasse (House
of the Hunt) has an elegant colonnaded courtyard and a
sophisticated private baths complex.

Bulla Regia's two most impressive public buildings are
a small and beautifully preserved theatre with special
seating reserved for its most important citizens, and the
imposing Memmian Baths close to the site entrance. The
market square and forum
are flanked by the ruins of
two temples, to Isis and
Apollo whose priceless
collection of statues are
also now at the Musée du
Bardo. There is a small
museum at the entrance
to the site.

DID YOU KNOW?

The main road between Tunis and Bulla Regia largely
follows the Mejerda Valley, which became a bloody
battlefield during World War II. Hundreds of lives were
lost when British and American troops clashed with the
Germans at Mejez el Bab, about 40km east of Béja.

DOUGGA (▶ 16, TOP TEN)

JEBEL ICHKEUL NATIONAL PARK (▶ 19, TOP TEN)

TABARKA ✪✪✪

Tabarka is Tunisia's flagship resort on the north coast. During the late 1980s and early 1990s the Tunisian government invested heavily in the town, building an 18-hole golf course, marina and an international airport nearby. It is mainly used in summer, bringing in mostly German and Italian holidaymakers. Nestled beneath the Kroumirie Mountains which are still covered with cork oaks, pine and eucalyptus, the small fishing village is not without charm, offering a long, unspoilt stretch of sandy beach to the east of the centre and to the west, a series of small rocky coves. The area is developing a reputation as a water-sports centre with quality facilities for sailing, diving and windsurfing. Tunnels Reef (20 minutes by boat from Tabarka) is an extraordinary complex of tunnels, caves, caverns and gullies.

The town began life as a Phoenician settlement and prospered in Roman times as a trading port. Modern-day Tabarka was largely designed by the French, who also built the causeway connecting the island of Tabarka to the mainland. The focal point of the town is avenue Habib Bourguiba where most of the shops and restaurants are to be found. The old port has been expanded into a luxury marina, Porto Corallo, and across the water is a 16th-century Genoese fort which is being prepared to house a small archaeological collection. The **Musée du Liège** (Cork Museum) 2km outside town on the Ain Draham road explains the industry and sells souvenirs.

🗺 28A6

✉ 175km from Tunis

🍽 Hôtel les Mimosas (££), avenue Habib Bourguiba (▶ 92)

🚌 Up to six buses daily to Tunis

✈ Tabarka Airport, 14km east of town

ℹ avenue du 7-Novembre
☎ 78 673555
🕐 Summer: 7.30–7; winter: Mon–Sat 8.30–1, 3–5

♿ Few

❓ Tabarka Jazz Festival in Jul; World Music Festival in Aug

Musée du Liège
✉ 2km out of town towards Ain Draham
🕐 Tue–Sun, 7–1, 3–6 (8–noon, 2–5 winter)
♿ None
🎟 Free

🕂 28A6
✉ 180km west of Tunis
🕐 Open access
🍴 At Ghardimaou
🚌 To Ghardimaou and then taxi
♿ None
🎟 Free

🕂 28B6
✉ 30km southeast of Bizerte
🕐 Daily 8–7 (8.30–5.30 in winter)
🍴 Picnic tables provided
🚌 Regular bus services between Tunis and Bizerte; get off at the turning about 2km from the site
♿ None
🎟 Cheap

The site of Utica's public baths was huge, and much remains intact

THUBURNICA ★

Way out west, only 15km from the Algerian border, the Roman remains at Thuburnica are not exceptional, but the scenery is pretty impressive. The most intact remnant of the town is the beautiful Roman bridge crossing the bed of a river which carries the run-off from the surrounding hills in winter. This is still used to reach the ruins of the town itself. Visitors who know what they are looking for will see the remains of a couple of temples, a triumphal arch and parts of a two-storey mausoleum. At the top of the hill is a small Byzantine fort.

UTICA ★

Equidistant between Tunis and Bizerte, Utica is now 10km from the sea though in Roman times it was an important port and the capital of the province of Africa. Much of the old Roman city lies buried under the deep mud of the Mejerda river which has been silting up for the past thousand years. The most intact part of the Roman remains is around La Maison de la Cascade (the House of the Waterfall) which obviously belonged to a very wealthy private citizen. The courtyard fountain, which gave its name to the house, still has remarkable mosaics.

The ruins of Utica's once-massive public baths complex still give an idea of how impressive they must once have been. Just in front of the entrance to the site there is a small museum containing pottery and other objects found at the baths.

Tunis to Jebel Ichkeul

An absorbing full-day itinerary which combines an unspoilt nature reserve and Roman ruins with one of the most striking and atmospheric towns in the country.

Head northwest out of Tunis on the P7 Tabarka road, through Jedeida to Mateur. Turn right towards Tinja and Menzel Bourguiba, following the signs to Lac Ichkeul.

The road becomes a track near the entrance to the park and at the gate visitors are asked to sign an official form (in French) promising to treat the countryside with respect.

From the gate, it is another 3km to the car park for the Eco Museum and the starting point for various walks (▶ 19). Leave the park following signs for Bizerte. After 15km, take the turning to Menzel Bourguiba, the former French garrison town of Ferryville.

The town was founded at the end of the 19th century to house European immigrants. Once nicknamed 'Little Paris', it has lost much of its charm but is worth a short stop on the way.

Return to the main Mateur–Bizerte road at the village of Tinja.

Fishermen can usually be seen battling to stop eel and mullet finding a way through the mesh of nets from Jebel Ichkeul to the open sea.

Head 20km north to Bizerte (▶ 40), the largest town on the north coast. Leave Bizerte on the A8 Tunis road. After 30km, there is a sign to the old Roman city of Utica (▶ 44). From Utica it is another 30km back to the centre of Tunis.

Distance
180km

Time
8 hours including several stops

Start/end point
Tunis
✚ 28B6

Lunch
🍴 Le Sport Nautique (£££)
✉ Boulevard Habib Bogatfa, Bizerte
☎ 72 431495

An atmospheric view of Lac d'Ichkeul, the heart of the Jebel Ichkeul National Park

Cap Bon

Standing slightly apart from the rest of the country, the peninsula which ends at Cap Bon is the most productive in Tunisia. With a year-round mild climate, it is known as the Garden of Tunisia; there are citrus and olive groves, and vineyards – although this is a Muslim country there is a long tradition of wine-making, and a wine festival at Grombalia during the autumn grape harvest.

On old maps of Tunisia, the town of Nabeul is given as the focal point of the region. It remains the largest town and seat of local government, but in recent years it has been eclipsed by the relentless expansion of near-neighbour Hammamet – the most cosmopolitan resort in Tunisia and a firm favourite with package holidaymakers from all over Europe. In contrast, on Cap Bon's northern coast there are many small villages and long stretches of deserted beach without a hotel in sight.

> *'The earliest navigators rounded Cap Bon and the glorious prospect of the Gulf of Tunis was unfolded before their eyes, the emerald waters being separated from the golden sand by a delicate edging of white surf'*

A. MACCALLUM SCOTT,
Tunis. A Medley of Races Under the French Flag (1921)

———————●———————

Original columns and mosaic floors at the winter baths of Thuburbo Majus

47

Hammamet

✚ 28C5
✉ 60 km southeast of Tunis
🚌 To Tunis and Nabeul
🚆 One train a day between Tunis and Hammamet
ℹ Avenue Habib Bourguiba
☎ 72 280423

Tunisia's largest resort has been attracting package holidaymakers since the 1960s. Less than an hour's drive from Tunis–Carthage airport and only slightly more than that from Monastir–Skanès airport (the main arrival point for charter flights), Hammamet is geared up to year-round tourism.

Easy-going and lively and with a good choice of restaurants, Hammamet's first hotels were built in the town centre close to the *médina* (➤ 49) but later developments stretch along the coast almost as far as Nabeul (➤ 52), making the most of some of the best beaches in the country. About 10km from the centre is the new resort of Hammamet Yasmine with a marina and good hotels.

The swimming pool of Sebastian's Villa, framed by whitewashed arches

What to See in Hammamet

CENTRE INTERNATIONAL CULTUREL   ✪✪

✉ Avenue des Nationes Unies
☎ 72 280410
🕐 8.30–6 (9–5 in winter)
♿ None
💲 Cheap
❓ Festival of the Arts, Jul, Aug

Built by millionaire George Sebastian in the 1920s, Sebastian's Villa was described by Frank Lloyd Wright as 'the most beautiful in the world'. Guests have included Winston Churchill, Anthony Eden and the artist Paul Klee; Rommel used it as his headquarters during World War II. Its open-air theatre stages an annual cultural festival each July and August and the building itself is a venue for conferences and art exhibitions.

DAR HAMMAMET   ✪

✉ The *médina*
☎ 72 281206
🕐 9–6
♿ None
💲 Moderate

A small museum in the *médina* (➤ 49), filled with traditional costumes and a selection of bridal dowries from various parts of the country. The jewellery and embroidery are particularly impressive. There is a fine view of the modern town and the old *médina* from the rooftop terrace.

Hammamet's médina is an atmospheric place to wander and shop

KASBAH ✪✪

First built in the 15th century but heavily modified and restored since, the Kasbah is the best place to begin a tour of the *médina* (➤ below). The fort is Hammamet's most conspicuous landmark and is entered by way of a colossal ramp. There are steep steps up to the ramparts, from where there are fine views over the white domes and terraces of the *médina* and the surrounding coastline.

✉ The *médina*
🕐 8–7 (9–5 in winter)
🍴 On the ramparts, the Café Turk (£)
♿ None
💷 Cheap

MÉDINA ✪✪✪

Much smaller than the *médinas* of Tunis (➤ 34), Sousse (➤ 62) and Sfax (➤ 73), but not without its charms, Hammamet's old town nestles around the Kasbah and Grande Mosquée (Great Mosque). It was built between 1463 and 1474 on the site of a 9th-century settlement. Although the streets closest to the *médina* walls are lined with souvenir shops there is a residential area which remains almost completely unspoilt. Wander through the narrow alleys – it's almost impossible to get lost. The studs on the doors are all individually designed and many incorporate the good luck symbols of fish and the hand of Fatima (the daughter of the Prophet Muhammed).

Immediately in front of the *médina* there is a market, and to the east is an ancient Muslim cemetery.

🍴 Café Sidi Bou Hdid, at the foot of the *kasbah* (➤ 94)
♿ None

PUPPUT ✪

Hammamet's only archaeological site consists of a couple of large Roman villas and a bath house paved with some fine mosaic floors. There are also 4th-century Christian tomb mosaics displayed on a perimeter wall. The ruins are all from the 2nd to the 4th centuries, when Pupput was a prosperous port.

✉ 6km south of the town centre
🕐 9–7 (to 5 in winter)
🚌 No public transport
💷 Cheap

The Ghar el Kebir caves near El Haouaria

28C6
✉ 14km northwest of Kerkouane
🍴 La Daurade (££)
   ✉ On the seashore
   ☎ 72 269080
❓ Festival of falconry (end of May–Jun)

28C6
✉ 68km northeast of Hammamet
🍴 Restaurant Anis (£–££)
   ✉ avenue Erriadh
   ☎ 72 295777

28C6
✉ 9km north of Kélibia
☎ 02 294033
🕐 Daily 9–9 (9–4 in winter). Museum closed Mon
🚌 Bus from Kélibia or taxi
♿ None
💰 Inexpensive

28C6
✉ 48km east of Tunis
🍴 Résidence des Thermes has a restaurant (££); Restaurant Dhib (£–££)
🚌 Bus from Tunis
♿ None

What to See in the Cap Bon region

EL HAOUARIA   ✪✪
Just outside the village of El Haouaria are the spectacular Ghar el-Kebir (Roman Caves). On the seafront directly opposite the island of Zembra, there are 24 caves which were quarried for the soft orange limestone used by Carthaginian, Roman and Byzantine builders and sculptors. South of the town is Haouria Plage, an amazing sheltered stretch of white sands.

KÉLIBIA   ✪✪
Kélibia is a busy working town with a picturesque fishing port, still unspoilt by tourism and a good base for exploring the Cap Bon region. Overlooking the town is the giant Fort of Kélibia which was built in the 16th century. The ramparts offer excellent views over the harbour, coastline and surrounding countryside. Kélibia's best beach is 2km north of the town at Mansourah.

KERKOUANE   ✪✪
Dating from the 4th century BC, Kerkouane is a remarkable survival of a purely Punic town. It was destroyed in 236 BC and unearthed in 1952; it is now listed as a UNESCO World Heritage Site. Many of the houses had private bathrooms. The little museum has some beautiful jewellery, funerary statues and pottery.

KORBOUS   ✪
A small spa town where people have come to 'take the waters' since Roman times. There are five springs including the hot and sulphurous Aïn el-Atrous (goat spring), said to be good for skin complaints and rheumatism. Women regularly slide down the nearby Zarziha Rock as a cure for infertility.

A Walk Around Nabeul

This leisurely walk offers an easy introduction to Nabeul (▶ 52–3).

Start at the Giant Orange Bowl on avenue Habib Thameur, a monument to the town's ceramic industry. Go past the regional hospital on the left before reaching the junction of avenue Farhat Hached and avenue Habib Bourguiba. Cross into avenue Farhat Hached.

The lanes of the covered souq lead to the Great Mosque

This is a busy shopping street packed with shops and stalls selling everything from jeans and T-shirts to leather bags and suitcases.

Follow the road round to the left and after 150m turn left again into the covered souq. *Walk through to emerge facing one of the elaborate entrances to Nabeul's Grande Mosquée (Great Mosque).*

Non-Muslims are barred from entry but walk round to the front for a glimpse of the courtyard. Note also the pretty tiled frontage of the house to the left of the mosque.

Cross the square, turn right into rue Souk el Ghezel and then right again into rue de France. With the Neapolis Center on the left, walk down the street and as you approach place des Martyrs – a formal public square with a fountain – turn left and through the gates of the bustling Marche Central.

The town's market is a riot of colour, sights and smells.

Return to place des Martyrs, turn left back into rue de France. After 250m head right into avenue Hedi Chaker, follow the road for 1km until a right-hand fork leads into rue Mohamed T'Latli and return to the Giant Orange Bowl.

Distance
3km

Time
2 hours allowing for shopping and drinks at the end

Start/end point
Giant Orange Bowl, Nabeul
✚ 28C5

Drinks
Café Errachida (£)
✉ Avenue Habib Thameur
🕐 All day

28C5

65km southeast of Tunis

Half-hourly to Tunis and Hammamet; depart from bus station on avenue Habib Thameur

avenue Taieb Mehiri
☎ 72 286800;
www.nabeul.net

Neapolis

Opposite Hotel Monia Club, just off the *route Touristique*

8–1, 4–7 (9.30–4.30 in winter). Closed Mon

None

Cheap

The popular Friday market in Nabeul

NABEUL ★★★

Nabeul used to be known simply as Tunisia's pottery town but it has rapidly developed as a resort in its own right with a clutch of large beachfront hotels. The main streets are crammed with pottery shops, souvenir stores and clothing boutiques, and every Friday the heart of the town is blocked off as Nabeul plays host to the so-called Camel Market. The huge market attracts busloads of tourists from everywhere and a large part of it is dedicated to crafts and souvenirs – you are unlikely to come across any real camels, though. For non-tourist goods the Marche Central (Central Market, ➤ 51) is much more genuine and well worth a visit.

In Roman times Nabeul's major industry was the manufacture of a pungent fish sauce called *garum* which was made by salting the blood and guts of tuna fish and then leaving it in an airtight container for three or four months. During excavations at Roman **Neapolis** on the outskirts of town during the 1960s several amphorae of the sauce were unearthed – but they appear to have passed their sell-by date. Neapolis is something of a disappointment if you have visited any of Tunisia's major archaeological sites – there is not much to see apart from a few pillars, some mosaic fragments and a series of pits thought to be the remains of a fish processing factory. The most colourful mosaics are on display at the interesting **Regional Museum**, as well as Carthaginian finds from the Cap Bon region. These include sculptures of the Carthaginian moon goddess Tanit unearthed in 1948 from a temple called Thinissut in the hills above Hammamet, some Carthaginian pieces excavated from Kerkouane, and a 2,500-year-old statue of a naked man and a collection of Roman domestic pottery.

Nabeul's pottery industry also dates back to Roman times with many of today's designs and popular colours (blue and white, and yellow and green) the same as those used 2,000 years ago. Although pottery can be bought all over Tunisia Nabeul offers one of the biggest selections. Tourists who hate the idea of haggling can shop for pots and plates at two official tourist shops in the town (▶109) where all goods have fixed prices. (Even if you like the idea of haggling it is worth calling in at one of the shops just to get an idea of the true cost of items.) Do not be fooled by one or two other shops in the town displaying signs which suggest they too have set prices. It is just a ploy to entice visitors in – you will then find prices become surprisingly flexible.

Nabeul is a thriving centre for the manufacture of bricks and perfume, the suburb of Dar Chaabane specialises in stone carving and the village of Beni Khiar 2km to the east is known for its carpet weaving and wool products.

The highly decorative Nabeul pottery is produced in many shapes and sizes

Archaeological Museum
- ✉ 44 avenue Habib Bourguiba
- ☎ 72 285509
- 🕐 8–1, 4–7 (9:30–4:30 in winter). Closed Mon
- 💶 Cheap

THUBURBO MAJUS ✪✪

First settled in the 5th century BC, most of the ruins at Thuburbo Majus are from later Roman times when the town was an important trading centre for the region's agricultural produce and probably had a population of around 8,000. Like many of Tunisia's archaeological sites, it is not unusual to have the place almost completely to yourself. With no guides available, even if you have a map, it can be quite difficult to make sense of the sprawling site.

The paved open space at the centre is the forum, which was where political and financial matters were discussed; the temple, built in AD 168, was dedicated to Jupiter, Juno and Minerva; the Winter Baths with their veined pink marble columns are up the hill. The Palaestra of the Petronii was a gymnasium (delineated by a line of columns) where young men took part in boxing or wrestling bouts. Many of the best finds from this site, including a statue of Jupiter and some fine mosaics, are now in the Musée du Bardo in Tunis (▶ 23, Top Ten).

➕ 28B5
✉ 60km southwest of Tunis, 65km west of Hammamet
🕐 Daily 8–7 (8.30–5.30 in winter)
🚌 From Tunis to El Fahs and then taxi
🖐 Inexpensive

Below: *The extensive Roman ruins,*
inset: *A relief of Pegasus*

ZAGHOUAN ✪

A sleepy, unspoilt agricultural town between Hammamet and Thuburbo Majus, with cobbled streets and tiled roofs. Dating from Roman times, water from Mount Zaghouan was used to supply Carthage by way of a 70km aqueduct, parts of which can still be seen along the Tunis–Zaghouan road. The Temple des Eaux (Temple of the Waters) built by Emperor Hadrian in AD 130 is the town's greatest sight.

➕ 28B5
✉ 30km west of Hammamet
🍴 Café at Temple des Eaux (£)
🚌 Frequent buses from Tunis, Nabeul and Hammamet

From Hammamet to Thuburbo Majus

An opportunity to combine spectacular Roman ruins with some unspoilt Tunisian countryside.

Head out of Hammamet on the main road towards Tunis. At the junction with the motorway follow the Zaghouan sign. On the outskirts of Zaghouan (➤ 54) follow signs for 'Centre Ville' turning left at the pharmacy and driving up the steep hill to the old town. Follow signs for Hôtel les Nymphes, turning right at Club de Chasse.

The Temple des Eaux (➤ 54) is surrounded by 12 empty niches which used to hold statues depicting the months of the year.

Turn left following signs to Tunis and El Fahs. After 12 km, immediately after the 'Welcome to El Fahs' sign, turn right and then left following the signs for Thuburbo Majus.

Allow at least an hour to look round the site (➤ 54).

Turn right out of the site, turning left after 1km on to the main Tunis road. Drive through the village of Bir M'Cherga and soon after take the right fork. After 25km, there is a right-hand turning towards Oudna.

Jebel Zaghouan stands high above the surrounding country

As you pass by note the well-preserved remains of the Roman aqueduct, which carried water from Zaghouan to Carthage.

After 6km turn right towards Mornag. Follow signs to Grombalia, crossing a rickety metal bridge only big (and safe) enough for one vehicle at a time. Turn right after 3km and follow signs for Bouficha. Just after the village of Oued Ezzit turn left towards Hamman Jedidi and the road back to Hammamet.

Distance
200km

Time
7–8 hours including stops

Start/end point
Hammamet
 28C5

Lunch
Picnic lunch at Thuburbo Majus or beside the Roman aqueduct at Oudna

Food & Drink

Tunisian cuisine is typically North African and is influenced by Islamic traditions as well as by its Berber culture, using powerful spices and plenty of vegetables and fish. The French colonial heritage has produced some excellent wines.

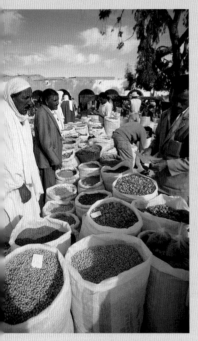

Dried beans and peas of many varieties are a staple part of Tunisian cuisine

Although international food is served in most Tunisian tourist hotels many holidaymakers will want to try at least some local cuisine. The Arabs, Turks and French have all had an influence on the country's cooking. Fish is given pride of place on any menu and restaurant owners compete with each other to display the freshest catch. Bream, grouper, sea bass and red mullet are among the most widely available, while seafood speciality dishes are based on prawns, lobster and squid. Tuna is added to everything – even when you ask for a vegetarian pizza or green salad! Eggs are another staple ingredient which appear unexpectedly in many dishes.

A Typical Tunisian Meal

In all but the cheapest restaurants customers are nearly always welcomed with complimentary *hors d'oeuvres* which may be as simple as a bowl of black olives and some delicious crusty bread. In most places the bread will also be accompanied with a small saucer of fiery red *harissa* paste made from hot chillies (caution is advised).

A very popular starter is the famous *brik*, a unique Tunisian dish which consists of a triangular-shaped envelope of crispy pastry containing a lightly cooked egg and often topped with fresh herbs, prawns or – of course – tuna. It can only really be eaten with the fingers but beware of the yolk making a sudden and undignified escape. Safer starters include *ojja*, which are scrambled eggs mixed with tomatoes, pimentos, peppers and garlic. *Mechouia* consists of diced onions, red peppers and tomatoes mixed with olive oil, grilled and then served with hard-boiled eggs and tuna. *Chorba* is a spicy soup of tomatoes, onions and *harissa* with wheat.

The obvious main course is *couscous*, a tasty vegetable, meat or fish stew served on a bed of steamed semolina grains, Tunisia's national dish. *Mesfuf* is a sweet *couscous* made with nuts and raisins. *Mechoui* (not to be confused with *mechouia*) is a plate of grilled meat, typically

Makroud, *a sweet and sticky pastry filled with dates, is a Kerouan speciality*

lamb chops with liver and *merguez* sausages generously laced with chilli.

Dessert is often a choice of fresh fruit or very sweet pastries like *baklava* (pastry with nuts and honey) or *kab el ghazal* (a horn-shaped pastry filled with almonds).

What to Drink

Although Tunisia is a Muslim country alcohol is quite freely available in hotels and restaurants in Tunis and the main beach resorts. Bars outside hotels are male-dominated which may make women feel unwelcome. Two micro-breweries in Hammamet and Port-el-Kantoul make their own German-style beer, but most bars still only serve Celtia, which is particularly good when served icy-cold. Tunisian wines are generally pleasant to drink, with the best wines coming from the Cap Bon region. There are several new winemakers and quality is improving. Some of the best are the Sélian wines.

Tunisia's best-known spirits are *Thibarine*, a sweet, aromatic date liqueur and *boukha*, a fig brandy.

Couscous, *traditional in Berber cuisine, is now Tunisia's national dish*

Central Tunisia

The coast of central Tunisia is a booming holiday region, with the growing beach resorts of Sousse and Monastir. Sfax and Sousse are a delight with their ancient city walls, vibrant *souqs*, fascinating museums and thriving fishing ports. In the Islamic world their importance is overshadowed by Kairouan which is at the heart of the country in every sense. Tunisia's most holy city combines its spiritual role as a national centre for prayer and pilgrimage with the secular demands of its commercial carpet-making industry.

The surrounding richly fertile plain, known as the Sahel, stretches down the central east coast embracing the resorts of Mahdia and Monastir. Its vast numbers of olive trees have been the mainstay of the region's economy since Roman times. In contrast, the western Tell, once forested, is now a hauntingly desolate terrain only suitable for rough grazing. Its main attraction is the isolated Roman ruin of Sbeïtla.

> ' *We quenched our thirst with tea in order to proceed in the dignified manner fitting for discovering such marvels* '

PAUL KLEE
Describing his first trip to
Kairouan, 1914

●

Tourists can try their hand at parascending from the water's edge

✚ 28C5
✉ 143km from Tunis
✈ International airport at
  Monastir-Skanès,
  15km away
🚇 On the Tunis–Gabès line
🚉 To Monastir and Mahdia
🚌 Buses to south and north
ℹ 1 avenue Habib
  Bourguiba ☎ 73 225157
  🕐 7.30–7 (Mon–Thu
  8.30–1, 3–5.30, Sat–Fri
  8.30–1.30 in winter).
  Morning opening only Fri,
  Sat. Closed Sun
🍴 Plenty of choice (£–£££)

Sousse

Sousse used to be just an excursion destination for day trippers; now it is a busy holiday centre in its own right. Packed with atmosphere and hundreds of years of history, Tunisia's leading city beach resort offers good quality hotels, a wide choice of affordable restaurants and endless possibilities for shopping.

With Carthage (►36) and Utica (►44), Sousse was one of the Phoenicians' three great coastal cities, with the earliest archaeological finds dating from the 6th century BC. In the 7th century AD the city fell to Arab invaders who left it in ruins, but in 790 the foundations for a new city were laid, and many remnants of this time still survive today.

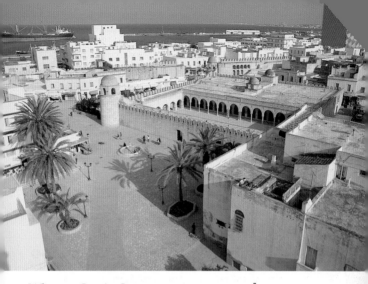

What to See in Sousse

CATACOMBS OF THE GOOD SHEPHERD ✪

The catacombs could be developed into a major tourist attraction but for the moment their appeal is limited. There are purported to be more than 15,000 marble tombs from the 2nd to the 5th centuries spread throughout a 5.5km network of tunnels but currently only one very small section is open to the public.

🕇 60A1 (arrowed)
✉ About 1km west of the *médina*, off rue Abdou Hamed el Ghazali
🕐 9–noon, 3–7 (9–noon, 2–6 in winter). Closed Mon
💵 Cheap

GRANDE BAIN MAURE SIDI BOURAOUI ✪✪

The Sidi Bouraoui Baths is one of the best places to try a traditional *hammam* or *bain maure* (Turkish bath) with lengthy separate sessions for men and women. In a country where not everyone has a private bathroom but where personal hygiene is taken very seriously the *hammam* plays an important role in Tunisian society. For tourists it offers an interesting insight into local culture, is a chance to meet local people and, most importantly, is a healthy, relaxing and pleasurable way to spend two or three hours. The masseur (or for women, a masseuse) uses a coarse glove known as a *tfal* which leaves the skin pink and tingling.

🕇 60B2
✉ Rue el Aghlaba (behind Mosquée Abd el Kader).
🕐 4am–3pm for men; 3pm–midnight for women
💵 Moderate

Above: *The beautiful city and historic port of Sousse*

GRANDE MOSQUÉE ✪✪✪

Respectful dress is required for a visit to the Great Mosque, which looks like a fortress with turrets and crenellations. Originally built in 851 by a freed slave called Mudam on the orders of the Aghlabite ruler Abdul Abbas, the internal courtyard has the pleasantly uncomplicated architecture common to many Islamic places of worship, the only decoration being a single line of Koranic inscription. A wide stairway leads to the walls; the minaret and prayer hall are not open to non-Muslims.

🕇 60C3
✉ Rue el-Aghlaba
🕐 Daily 8–2. Closes 8–1 Fri
♿ None
💵 Cheap

⊞ 60B1
⊠ Off boulevard Marechal Tito
🕐 Summer: Tue–Thu 9–noon, 3–7, Fri–Sun 9–6 (Tue–Thu 9–noon, 2–6, Fri–Sun 9–6 in winter). Closed Mon and public holidays
♿ None
💷 Moderate

⊞ 60B2
🍴 Many cafés (£)
♿ None

KASBAH SOUSSE MUSEUM

Situated in the southwest corner of the *médina* (►below) the Kasbah Sousse Museum not only offers a superb panoramic view across the city, but has a fine and most interesting collection of mosaics rivalling those at the Musée du Bardo (►23, Top 10). Most of the mosaics date from the 3rd and 4th centuries with the depiction of the Triumph of Bacchus among the most noted. The adjoining courtyard is a pleasant place to sit amongst the palm trees, flowers and bits of marble column and stone tablets.

MÉDINA

The *médina* is the old heart of Sousse and the area of the city with the greatest appeal. Its 9th-century walls are still largely intact apart from the area around the former sea gate at place des Martyrs, which was destroyed by the Allies during World War II – a testament to the continuing strategic importance of the city.

The *médina*'s biggest attractions are the Grande Mosquée (►61), the *ribat* (►63) and the Kasbah Museum (►above). Equally evocative and rewarding, however, is its overall ambience. Despite the increasing impact of tourism, the *médina* has retained a considerable amount of charm and character. The main shopping street runs from east to west from Bab Jedid to Bab el Gharbi. Halfway along, as the thoroughfare changes its name from rue Souq el Reba to rue Souq el Caïd, is a small warren of covered *souqs* selling everything from food and clothes to perfume and jewellery.

⊞ 52B2
⊠ Rue Souq el Reba
🕐 Mon–Thu, Sat 9.30–1, 3–5.30, Sun 10–2
♿ None
💷 Cheap

Above: *Haggling over souvenirs in the rue d'Angleterre in the médina of Sousse*

MUSÉE DE KALAOUT EL KOUBBA ✪

The Museum of Kalaout el Koubba is in one of the most unusual buildings in the *médina* (►above) with a striking zigzag decoration on the dome. Dating from around the 11th century and believed to have been either an audience chamber for a neighbouring Fatimid palace or one of the hot rooms of a *hammam*, it has had many uses in its time, most recently as an art gallery and café. Today the museum's displays focus on the traditional life of the *médina* with ceramics, kitchen equipment, musical instruments and national costumes.

The main gate and circular tower of the Byzantine ribat *in Sousse*

RIBAT ✪✪✪

The *ribat* was built early in the 9th century as one of a chain of fortresses stretching along the Mediterranean coast to defend North Africa from European invaders. It was completed by the Aghlabids in 821, incorporating an earlier structure built in 790 which itself was sited on the ruins of a 6th-century Byzantine fortress. The large central courtyard which slopes downwards to a cistern is surrounded by a series of small cells which were used by the warrior-monks as tiny study-bedrooms.

A room above the main gate has four slits in the floor through which boiling olive oil was poured on unwelcome visitors. For many visitors, though, the most interesting part of the *ribat* is the view from the ramparts over the *médina* (▶ 62). There is often a queue to climb the 75 steps to the top of the circular tower for views of the town.

🕂 60B3
⊠ Rue el Aghlaba
🕐 Daily 8–7 (8–5.30 in winter)
🕭 None
🖾 Cheap

DID YOU KNOW?

If you are in Sousse on a Sunday there is a large open-air market which sprawls endlessly along the Sousse–Sfax road and draws a huge crowd. It is said to be possible to buy anything from a car to a camel – although most people make rather smaller purchases.

From Sousse to El Jem

Distance
160km

Time
Seven hours including stops

Start/end point
Sousse
➕ 60C5

Lunch
Restaurant at Hotel Julius (£)
✉ Next to train station in El-Jem

This scenic drive includes the tourist town of Monastir (➤ 68) and is ideal for holidaymakers looking for a day trip from Sousse (or Port El Kantaoui, ➤ 70). Starting soon after breakfast is recommended.

Head southwest out of Sousse past the louages station following signs to Sfax and Kairouan. Drive through the suburbs of Zaouiet Sousse and Messadine. Soon after leaving M'Saken join the GP1 and head south on a long, straight road flanked by row upon row of olive trees.

It takes just over an hour to get to El Jem (➤ 17, Top Ten) driving at a leisurely pace. It is impossible to miss the amphitheatre which dominates the small town and can be seen clearly from the approach road. Finding somewhere to park may be more difficult. Allow a good 90 minutes for the amphitheatre and the Archaeological Museum.

From the museum turn left on avenue Taieb Mehini and continue along avenue Belhaouane, taking the MC87 to Mahdia. Drive for 10km passing through the village of Telelsa and then turn left at the signpost for Moknine, known for its pottery. Reaching a crossroads after about 12km head straight on into the village of El Fhoul, reaching Moknine 16km later. Follow the signs to Monastir 30km further north.

The *ribat* and Bourguiba Mausoleum are among Monastir's main tourist attractions (➤ 68–9). The town is also good for souvenir shopping.

Head out of town following signposts for Tunis. Take the A1 north for the easy 20km drive back to Sousse.

The extravagant mausoleum of Habib Bourguiba, seen from the tower of the ribat in Monastir

What to See in Central Tunisia

EL JEM (▶ 17, TOP TEN)

ILES KERKENNAH (▶ 18, TOP TEN)

KAIROUAN (▶ 20–1, TOP TEN)

LE KEF   ✪✪✪

Le Kef – which means 'rock' in Arabic – refers to the town's dramatic setting on a rocky outcrop just below the summit of Jebel Dyr. Considered to be the capital of the Tell region which covers much of Central Tunisia, Le Kef is Tunisia's most significant inland centre after Kairouan. This was a fortress town from 450 BC, and tools have been found in surrounding caves and woodland dating back 50,000 years. In Roman times Le Kef became an important trading post and over the last thousand years it has been involved in numerous border wars and disputes. During World War II it served as headquarters for the Free French.

Aïn el Kef is a spring which may well have been the reason for a town being built here; it has been venerated for centuries and a small shrine still attracts votive offerings. Le Kef has two *kasbahs* which are linked by a drawbridge and enclosed by a wall. The older, larger fort was first built in Byzantine times and later remodelled by the Turks; the other was built in the early 19th century. Jemaa el Kebir (Old Mosque) was one of the oldest mosques in Tunisia but is now closed. Next to it the Mosquée de Sidi Bou Makhlouf was built at the beginning of the 17th century and is named after the town's patron. The **Musée Regional des Arts et Traditions Populaires** (Regional Museum of Popular Arts and Traditions) focuses on the culture of the Berber people with displays of clothes, jewellery and household objects.

Below: The fortifications at Le Kef

🔲 28A5
✉ 170km southwest of Tunis
🚌 To Tunis from the Gare Routière SNT
ℹ The Artisanat Dar El Medina (The Association for the Protection of the Medina) acts as an informal tourist office:
   ✉ rue Hedi Chaker
🍴 Hotel-Restaurant Venus (££) ✉ Junction of rue Farhat Hached and avenue Habib Bourguiba
   ☎ 78 200355

Kasbahs
🕐 Daily 7–7. Closed Mon
💷 Free

Musée Regional des Arts et Traditions Populaires
✉ Place Ben Aissa
☎ 78 221503
🕐 9–1, 4.30–7 (9.30–4.30 in winter)
💷 Cheap

28C5

✉ 205km from Tunis, 62km from Sousse

🍴 Cafés in place du Caire (£)

🚆 One train a day to and from Tunis from the station on avenue Farhat Hached

🚌 Almost hourly buses to Sousse and Sfax

ℹ Rue el Moez (just inside the médina by the Skifa el-Kahla) ☎ 73 681098

♿ Few

Archaeological Museum

✚ Place de l'Indépendance

🕐 9–1, 3–7 (9–4 in winter). Closed Mon

♿ None

💰 Cheap

Borj el Kebir

✚ Rue du Borj

🕐 9–1, 3–7 (9–4 in winter). Closed Mon

♿ None

💰 Cheap

The entrance to the mosque in Mahdia

MAHDIA ✪✪

Set on a peninsula and still clinging to its old way of life, as much as it can, with its weaving industry and thriving fishing port, Mahdia's small *médina* is the most obvious sign of the town's changing fortunes. Nearly every shop and stall is now geared towards tourists since the creation of a burgeoning *zone touristique* 6km west of the town centre, where the best beaches are to be found.

Mahdia's history dates from the 10th century when it was the capital of the Fatimid dynasty. All that remains of the town's fortifications is the Skifa el-Kahla (the Dark Gate), which stands at the entrance to the *médina*. Next to it is the new **Archaeological Museum**, with exhibits from Punic, Roman and Fatimid times and a collection of traditional costumes.

Take a walk along the main thoroughfare, the rue Obaidallah el Mehdi. At the end of the street there is the picture-perfect place du Caire where cafés, some with seats shaded by trees and vines, serve refreshments throughout the day. Just beyond the square is the Grande Mosquée (Great Mosque), but do not be fooled by its aged appearance – it was built in the 1960s and is a replica of the thousand-year-old original. The large fortress which stands on the highest point of the peninsula is the **Borj el Kebir**, a 16th-century Turkish fort which offers excellent views over the town, port and surrounding Muslim cemetery. The port may look familiar: it was used as the setting for the German invasion of Benghazi in the Academy Award-winning film *The English Patient*.

A Walk Around Mahdia

This walk can be done at any time of the day but is particularly recommended in the early morning or late afternoon.

Start at the fishing harbour, which is still the focal point of Mahdia despite the onslaught of tourism.

Allow time to visit the harbour where fishermen unload the catch or repair their nets; call in at the slippery-floored fish market where they auction fish straight from the sea.

Turn right out of the harbour entrance on to the seafront path (rue du Borj) which leads to the Grande Mosquée (Great Mosque) and Borj el Kebir (► 66). With the fort on your left, branch off to walk through the cemetery with its simple white gravestones. Follow the path round to the tiny red lighthouse passing the gardens and rocks off to the right which form Cap d'Afrique. Turning the corner of the windswept headland, notice the whitewashed roofs of the zone touristique *in the distance. Walk back towards Mahdia town along rue 7 Novembre, with traditional seafront houses.*

You will pass the ASM (Association de Sauvegarde de Médina, ► 68) on the left in a grand old house, which offers information about the *médina* and renovation projects.

Turn left up the alleyway running alongside the Hotel Al-Jazira. Follow it around to emerge next to the tourist information centre and the main entrance to the médina. *Stroll down rue Obaidallah el Mehdi to the shaded place du Caire and then turn right by the side of Mosquée Mustapha Hamza which leads to a cluster of shops and cafés on rue des Fatmides.*

Distance
4km

Time
Two hours including stops

Start point
Fishing port
✚ 28C5

End point
Rue des Fatmides
✚ 28C5

Lunch or coffee
Restaurant de la Medina (£)
✉ Same building as fish
   market

The old port of Mahdia, protected by the lighthouse on Cap d'Afrique

Monastir

Until the 1960s Monastir was a fairly typical Tunisian town, but it has been transformed into a showpiece tourist resort of pristine streets, elegant turn of the century lampposts and an abundance of greenery. It has an attractive 400-berth marina and an old fishing port. Most of Monastir's tourist hotels are located 6km west of the town centre in the suburb of Skanès near the international airport.

✉ 160km south of Tunis

🚂 From Sousse

🚌 Frequent departures to Tunis and Sousse

ℹ Rue de l'Indépendance
  🕐 Mon–Sat 8–6. Closed Sun
  Also Monastir Airport
  ☎ 73 461205 🕐 24 hrs

❓ Monastir International Festival every summer; www.monastir.org

✉ Top end of Sidi el Mazeri Cemetery
🕐 Mon–Thu 2–4.30, Fri–Sun 9–4.30
🎟 Free

Above: *The massive* ribat *of Harthema stands above the harbour at Monastir*

What to See in Monastir

BOURGUIBA MAUSOLÉE ✪✪

In the early years of his presidency, the Republic of Tunisia's first leader Habib Bourguiba built himself an elaborate mausoleum here in the centre of the town of his birth. Instantly recognisable by its twin minarets and golden dome, it has an impressive tree-lined drive leading to the gates; at its foot is a kiosk commemorating those who died fighting for Tunisia's independence. A golden statue of the schoolboy Bourguiba stands in the nearby place du Gouvernorat.

Association de Sauvegarde de Médina
✉ Rue du 2 Mars
🕐 9–1, 3–7 (9–noon, 2–6 in winter). Closed Mon
❓ Special exhibitions occasionally mounted

MÉDINA ✪

A great chunk of Monastir's *médina* was demolished in the 1960s in the course of a misguided modernisation plan, and with it the Old Town district lost much of its heart. Dedicated to protecting the *médina* from any further development (a somewhat lost cause) is the **Association de Sauvegarde de Médina** (City Safe-Keeping Association). Its centre, built around a whitewashed courtyard shaded by an orange tree, provides a welcome oasis from the surrounding bustle.

MUSÉE DU COSTUME TRADITIONNEL ✪✪

Refurbished in 1996, the stone-floored, somewhat spartan Museum of Traditional Costume contains a collection of impressive outfits worn by couples on their wedding day – and for many days following the ceremony. In the 18th and 19th centuries it was traditional for the bride's dress to be made by her mother and sisters, which sometimes took several years because of the huge amount of intricate embroidery involved. The men's costumes are much simpler. The costumes are attractively presented in glass-fronted cabinets, with a display of costume jewellery.

✉ Avenue de l'Indépendance
🕐 Summer: 9–1, 4–7; winter: 9–4. Closed Mon
💶 Cheap

RIBAT ✪✪✪

Founded in 796, the *ribat* has been reworked and restored so many times that there is little left of the original structure. One surviving section from earliest times is the prayer hall which is now used as a **Museum of Islamic Arts**. Exhibits include fragments of 12th-century weaving, Egyptian fabrics, samples of Islamic writings and a gold jewellery collection from Persia. The Nador tower offers spectacular views over the town centre and corniche.

The *ribat* has provided the backdrop for scenes in several major films including *Jesus of Nazareth* and *The Life of Brian*. Connected to the southern gate is the Grande Mosquée (Great Mosque), built at the same time as the *ribat* and *médina* walls. It is closed to non-Muslims.

✉ Behind the route de la Corniche
☎ 73 461272
🕐 8–7 (8–5.30 in winter)
💶 Cheap (includes entry to Museum of Islamic Arts)

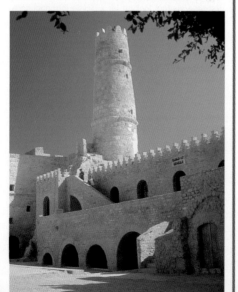

The Nador tower gives spectacular views over Monastir

69

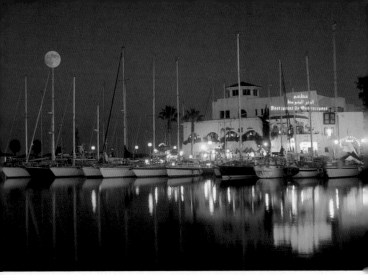

+ 28C5
⊠ 134km south of Tunis
🚌 Buses to Sousse operate
along the main road just
outside the entrance to
Port El Kantaoui
ℹ The marina ⏰ Summer:
daily 7.30–7; winter
Mon–Sat 8–6, closed Sun
🍴 Large choice of
restaurants (£–£££)

Above: *The recently built
resort town of El Kantaoui
is focused on the marina*

PORT EL KANTAOUI ★★

Port El Kantaoui arouses quite strong feelings between
those who love the resort and those who are rather less
keen. Purpose-built around a picturesque marina which
now draws luxury yachts from all over the world, it opened
in 1979 and has been Tunisia's most outstandingly
successful tourist centre.

With the look and feel of an elite residential district, it is
the sort of development where you would expect to find
the homes of top politicians, diplomats or the fabulously
wealthy. The only difference is that the residents of this
smart enclave are mainly package holidaymakers, often
first-time visitors looking for a gentle introduction to
Tunisia. Equally popular with families and older couples
who like its reassuringly familiar ambience and strong
sense of safety, detractors criticise Port El Kantaoui for its
artificiality. It's also not unusual to find holidaymakers
outnumbering Tunisians ten to one.

Millions of dinars have been poured into landscaping,
with palm trees, shrubs and grass borders lining every
road and not a tatty bit of paintwork in sight. The resort's
hotels are equally sparkling; giant whitewashed palaces
with their own terraced gardens awash with
bougainvillaea.

> ### DID YOU KNOW?
>
> If you want to get from Port El Kantaoui to Sousse and
> don't want to take a taxi, you can ride in an open-sided
> 'Noddy Train' which is very popular with children. It
> operates hourly daytime services between the two
> resorts, leaving from the main entrance to the Kantaoui
> marina in front of the imitation fort.

The early built hotels have the advantage of being closest to the marina and are also generally thought to offer the best quality. Some of the newest accommodation can involve a good ten-minute walk to the shops and restaurants surrounding the harbour. Port El Kantaoui is practically self-sufficient and apart from the obligatory souvenir shops it has banks, a supermarket, hairdressers and a newsagent.

Sailing trips in glass-bottomed cruisers, fishing boats or in an imitation pirate's galleon are available from the marina. There is also a diving club and nearby riding stables have horses and camels for hire. Port El Kantaoui's pride and joy is its beautifully manicured 36-hole championship golf course (➤ 113). There are no membership requirements and while golfers with their own equipment are welcome, those who prefer to travel light can hire everything from clubs to caddies at very reasonable rates. Most hotels will arrange bookings and pre-set tee-times with the club.

The Temple of Jupiter catches the evening sun at Sufetula near Sbeïtla

SBEÏTLA ★★

If it were not for its impressive Roman ruins, Sbeïtla would attract very few visitors. Far from any tourist resort, Sbeïtla is the most southerly of Tunisia's major Roman sites. Established at the beginning of the first century on what had been an early Numidian settlement, it was known as Sufetula and reached the height of its prosperity towards the end of the 2nd century. By then it had a population of more than 10,000 people, double the number of people who live in Sbeïtla today.

There is a massive triumphal arch just before the entrance to the archaeological site; other interesting ruins include the much-photographed forum built in AD 139, the well-preserved baths with their ingenious under-floor heating system and a more modern structure, the 6th-century Basilica of St Vitalis with a beautiful baptismal font covered in mosaics.

✚ 28C5
✉ 117km west of Kairouan
🕐 7–7 (8.30–5.30 in winter)
🚌 Three buses a day to Kairouan from a car park on the southern edge of town, off rue Habib Thameur
♿ None
✋ Moderate

Sfax

Tunisia's second city is rarely visited by holiday-makers except perhaps those with a couple of hours to spare while awaiting ferries to Iles Kerkennah (► 18). Although it is mainly an industrial city with factories sprawling along the coastline, the city centre is attractively compact and very underrated. One of the joys of Sfax is being able to wander through its streets and *souqs* without hassle from over-eager traders.

Founded in 849 near the site of a small Roman town, Taparura, Sfax quickly became prosperous by trading in the products of the Sahel's olive trees. Remaining largely independent until the beginning of the 17th century it strongly resisted the imposition of the French Protectorate in 1881 which led to French marines storming the city defacing its mosques and killing several hundred people. Hedi Chaker and Farhat Hached, two of the Tunisia's trade union leaders involved in securing the country's independence and whose names are seen on street signs across the country, both hailed from Sfax.

What to See in Sfax

ARCHAEOLOGICAL MUSEUM   ✪
The archaeological collection is housed on the ground floor of the Town Hall, an unmistakable colonial building with a dome and clock tower. Although it only comprises six exhibition rooms there are several items of interest including an unusual 3rd-century Roman mosaic of children wrestling, Christian funerary mosaics and Roman and Muslim tombs. There are also displays of Roman wall paintings, glass and prehistoric tools from Gafsa (► 83).

- ✚ 28C4
- ✉ 270km southeast of Tunis
- 🚆 Five services a day (four in winter) to El Jem, Sousse and Tunis from the station at the eastern end of avenue Habib Bourguiba.
- 🚌 To Tunis and Sousse
- ⛴ Regular daytime services to Iles Kerkennah
- ✈ Four Tuninter flights a week to Tunis
- ℹ La Corniche ☎ 74 497041 ◙ Mon–Thu 8.30–1, 3–5.45, Fri–Sat 8.30–1.30
- ❓ Socopa Craft Shop ✉ rue Hammadi Taj ☎ 74 296826 ◙ 9–noon, 4–7 (9–noon, 3–6 in winter)

Above: *The massive defensive walls of the old town of Sfax*

- ✉ Junction of avenues Habib Bourguiba and Hedi Chaker
- ☎ 74 229744
- ◙ Mon–Sat 8.30–1, 3–6
- 💷 Cheap

MÉDINA ●●●

The old town in Sfax has one of the best-preserved and most atmospheric *médinas* in the country. Surrounded by massive stone walls originally built by the Aghlabites in the 9th century, it is a hive of activity with dozens of first-floor workshops for tailors, engravers and furniture-makers. At the heart of a labyrinth of narrow streets and *impasses* is the Grande Mosquée (Great Mosque), which was started in 849 and extensively rebuilt in the 10th century. Closed to non-Muslims, the best view of its celebrated, several-tiered minaret is from place Souk el Djemaa.

Sfax's covered *souqs* run between the Grande Mosquée and rue des Forgerons. Immediately beyond Bab Jebli, the oldest surviving gateway to the *médina*, is a large food market. Go early in the day as the night's fishing catch is unloaded from cold storage vans. An even bigger daily fish market operates opposite the docks on avenue Ali Bach Hamba.

✉ Main entrance on avenue Ali Belhouane
🍴 Many cafés (£)
👆 Free

MUSÉE REGIONAL DES ARTS ET TRADITIONS ●●

The Regional Museum of Arts and Traditions (also known as the Dar Jallouli museum), is at the heart of the *médina* in a handsome 17th century townhouse, the former home of one of Tunisia's most influential families, and gives an idea of what life would have been like for an upper class family in Sfax in the 19th century. The house itself is just as interesting as the exhibits, with its white paved floors, tiled walls and carved wood ceilings. As well as displays of furniture, traditional costumes and jewellery, there are special sections on calligraphy and painting on glass.

✉ Rue de le Driba
☎ 74 211186
🕐 9–4.30. Closed Mon
👆 Cheap

Below: *Narrow alleyways honeycomb the* médina *in Sfax*

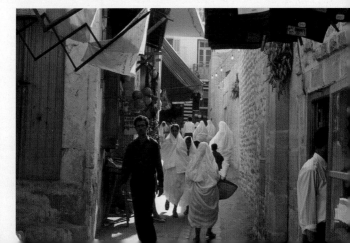

In the Know

If you want to get the real flavour and feel of the country, here are some ideas.

10
Ways to Be a Local

Learn a few words of Arabic – it works wonders and is well worth the effort for the obvious pleasure it brings.

Avoid talking politics or criticising the President, whose photograph appears everywhere.

Sweat it all out at the *hammam*, the Turkish bath, and get scrubbed by a masseur for extra cleanliness.

Buy a *burnous* – a long woollen coat with a hood which is very useful in the winter when it can turn extremely cold in the north.

Smoke a *chicha* (hookah pipe filled with flavoured tobacco) while playing a game of cards in a smoky, starkly lit café or bar.

Never switch on your car headlights until it is pitch black assuming that because you know you are on the road everyone else must be able to see you.

Get up at sunrise and consider you are having a late night if you are still out on the town at 10pm.

Eat your couscous, the classic North African dish, hot and spicy.

Be prepared for the incessant ringing of mobile phones; conversations will be conducted at a decibel level which would seem to make their use superfluous.

Be prepared to haggle – bargaining is a way of life throughout the Arab world and, with the exception of medicine, applies to just about all commercial transactions. Start your bidding with a price under what you are willing to pay.

10
Good Places to Have Lunch

Restaurant Bon Kif (££–£££) avenue Marbella (off avenue Habib Thameur), Nabeul ☎ 72 222783. Stylish Tunisian restaurant where tourists and locals gather for long, lazy lunches.

Fishing from a small boat is a way of life for many Tunisians

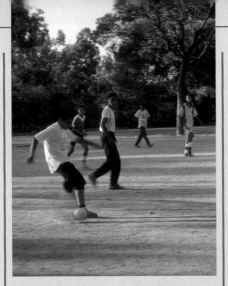

Boys enjoy a game of football in Belvedere Park, Tunis

Golf Very high standards and eight courses to choose from.
Sand skiing with narrow skis off the sand dunes near Douz.
Watersports Try waterskiing, paragliding and windsurfing in all the main beach resorts.

10
Places to Picnic

- Jebel Ichkeul National Park (► 19)
- Thuburbo Majus (► 54)
- Any of the deserted beaches on Iles Kerkennah (► 18)
- Parc du Belvédère, Tunis (► 35)
- The empty roadside near the desert villages of Chebika, Midès and Tamerza (► 82, 85, 86)
- Dougga (► 16)
- Bulla Regia (► 42)
- Carthage (► 26, 36)
- Sbeïtla (► 71)
- Thuburnica (► 44)

Chez Achour (££) rue Ali Belhouane, Hammamet ☎ 72 280140. The best fish and seafood in town.
Dar Chakra (£–££) In a courtyard after Tourist Office, Monastir ☎ 73 460528. Very good Tunisian dishes served in a beautifully restored old house.
Dar El Jeld (£££) rue Dar El Jeld, Tunis ☎ 71 560916. Superb Tunisian food in a sumptuous mansion.
La Daurade (££–£££) The Marina, Port El Kantaoui ☎ 73 348893. Very popular fish restaurant with shaded outside seating.
Le Lido (££) avenue Mohammed V, Sousse ☎ 73 225329. Sit outside opposite the harbour and enjoy fresh fish.
Le Neptune (££) 123 rue de Haffoux, Sfax ☎ 74 212890. Elegant room and good service, plus some of the best food in town.
Le Petit Navire (££) avenue du 7-Novembre, Mahdia ☎ 73 681927. Superb fish restaurant with sea views on the terrace.
Restô (£££) Villa Didon, Carthage ☎ 71 733433. Stylish restaurant with

excellent Mediterranean dishes.
Le Sport Nautique (£££) boulevard Habib Bougatfa, Bizerte ☎ 72 433262. Ideal for a leisurely lunch overlooking the entrance to the harbour.

10
Top Activities

Bathing Most Tunisians visit a *hammam* (Turkish bath) at least once a week.
Cinema-going A very popular pastime, even though most films are dubbed and long films heavily cut.
Cycling No better place than on the flat, uncrowded roads of Iles Kerkennah.
Diving Quality tuition and excellent dive sites in the waters around Tabarka.
Fishing A way of life for many Tunisians; no permit is required to fish from any of the harbours.
Football Tunisians are fanatical about football at all levels with Sunday the big day for local matches.
Four-wheel driving Ideal transport for exploring the desert region.

A poster advertising an Egyptian film; cinema-going is very popular

Jerba & the South

Apart from Jerba which offers some of the most unspoilt beaches in the Mediterranean and a charming pocket-sized capital, Houmt Souq, the desert region remains a well-kept secret. Covering much of the southern half of the country, it is beginning to attract a little more attention since the worldwide success of the Oscar-winning movie *The English Patient*, much of which was filmed around the oasis town of Tozeur. European holidaymakers usually prefer to visit the desert region in early spring or late autumn as the summer months can be oppressively hot.

Desert safaris from the east coast beach resorts rarely stay more than two or three nights in the region, with Tozeur the traditional focal point. Popular spots en route include Matmata with its unusual cave dwellings made famous in another big movie, *Star Wars*, and the Gorges de Selja, famous for the rail journey on Le Lézard Rouge (Red Lizard) train.

> *' I slipped into the orchards and experienced the cheerfulness of the fountains amidst the blossoming trees. '*

SIMONE DE BEAUVOIR
(1908–86) on seeing the oasis
at Gabès.

─────●─────

The dramatic gorge of Midès in the far southwest

28C3

506km south of Tunis

Two to four services a day to Sousse, Sfax and Tunis

Up to seven Tuninter flights a day from Jerba to Tunis from Mellita airport

place des Martyrs, Houmt Souq 75 650915 Summer: Mon–Sat 8.30–1; winter: Mon–Thu 8.30–1, 3–5.45, Fri–Sat 8.30–1

Above: *A shady square in Houmt Souq, the main town on the island of Jerba*

22km south of Houmt Souq

To Jorf every 30 minutes, 6am–9pm; every 2 hours, 9pm–6am

Cheap for cars; free for foot passengers

7km long from southeast corner of Ile de Jerba to the mainland

Free

Jerba

Thought to be the 'land of the Lotus Eaters', where Ulysses came ashore during his Odyssey, Jerba is the holiday destination of many Tunisians. It is the only beach resort in the country which can claim to be attractive year-round, though it can be quite chilly during the day from November to January with the temperature dropping further at night.

While its population of 120,000 is one of the most cosmopolitan in the country, Jerba society is deeply conservative and – confronted with the demands of foreign tourists – there remains a strong determination to preserve the island's distinct identity. Measuring just 29km wide by 27km long, Jerba is said to have 354 mosques – one for every day of the Islamic year.

What to See in Jerba

AJIM

Visitors arriving by ferry dock at Ajim. Still an important centre for sponges, which are collected from the seabed by divers, it is also a busy fishing port. In the summer months there can be long queues for the car ferry to Jorf – a two-hour wait is not unusual. Swimming around Ajim is not recommended, as there are often swarms of jellyfish in this area, as well as octopuses.

EL KANTARA CAUSEWAY

Driving across the El Kantara Causeway is the alternative to taking the ferry to and from the mainland, but it adds around 100km to a journey. The first causeway was built in Carthaginian times and survived until 1551, when it was badly damaged by the Turkish pirate Dragut. Repairs were not made until 1953.

ERRIADH (HARA SEGHIRA) ✪

The only reason for coming here is to see the **El Ghriba Synagogue**, one of the most holy Jewish shrines in North Africa. There has been a strong Jewish presence in Tunisia, and particularly in Jerba, going back many centuries. Jerba's Jews today number around a thousand, many having migrated to Israel, and the synagogue now provides a meeting place for the ageing community. Suitably dressed visitors are welcome to enter the atmospheric synagogue with its bright blue pillars, dark wood panelling, painted tiles and stained glass.

✉ 8km from Houmt Souq
🚌 Buses from Houmt Souq to Guellala (► below) stop in Erriadh

El Ghriba Synagogue
✉ 1km from town centre
🕐 Sun–Thu 9.30–12.30, 2.30–5, Fri 9.30–2. Closed Sat
♿ None
🎟 Cheap

GUELLALA ✪✪

Guellala rivals Nabeul (► 52) as a pottery-producing centre. The clay for the pottery – all of which is handmade – is quarried from hills above the village and out towards nearby Sedouikech. The main street is lined with shops all piled high with pots and plates; there are several workshops and dozens of kilns. Haggle effectively and most pieces are very cheap, though quality varies enormously. Expect to pay more for anything with fish on it and look out for specialities such as camel-shaped jugs. Guellala is a popular morning stop on tours of the island, so the best bargains can usually be negotiated in mid-afternoon when there are fewer people around.

✉ 18km from Houmt Souq, 6km from El Kantara
🚌 Four buses a day from Houmt Souq
♿ None

Musée de Guellala
✉ 1km from town on the road to Sedouikech
☎ 75 761114
🕐 Jul–Aug 8am–11pm; Sep–Jun 8–8
🍴 Café-restaurant in the museum (£–££)
🎟 Moderate

Left: *A potter at work in Guellala*

The Mosquée de Guellala (1km out of town on the road to Erriadh) dates from the 15th century. The **Musée de Guellala** is a beautiful example of the local traditional architecture. The spacious rooms are filled with exhibits on the traditional way of life.

79

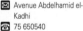

- ✚ 28C4
- ✉ 22km northeast of Ajim
- 🍴 Good choice (£–££)
- 🚌 Bus station on rue Mosbah–Jarbou with 4 buses a day to Tunis, Sousse, Sfax and buses around the island
- ✉ Boulevard de l'Environment
- ☎ 75 650016

Borj el Kebir

- ✉ At the seafront end of rue Taieb Mehiri, 700m from the fishing port
- 🕐 8–7 (9.30–4.30 in winter). Closed Fri
- 💰 Cheap

Musée des Arts et Traditions Populaires

- ✉ Avenue Abdelhamid el-Kadhi
- ☎ 75 650540
- 🕐 8–noon, 3–7 (9.30–4.30 in winter). Closed Fri
- 💰 Moderate

Above: *Carpet market*
Opposite, top: *Silver brooch from the museum*
Right: *Ancient olive tree near Midoun*

HOUMT SOUQ ⭐⭐⭐

Houmt Souq, the capital of Jerba, is situated on the island's north coast 6km from the airport at Mellita. It is a charming place to spend few days and makes a good base for excursions to other parts of the island and further afield. Houmt Souq means 'marketplace', and this remains the town's primary purpose despite its now blossoming tourism industry, which has brought the inevitable crop of souvenir shops and European-style restaurants.

The heart of the town is the snug little complex of whitewashed squares and streets surrounding the *souq*, where goods including jewellery, coral and leatherware are sold. There is also a daily fish auction. Mondays and Thursdays are the busiest days when traders come in from all over the island to sell straw baskets and mats.

On the seafront, close to Houmt Souq's busy fishing harbour, is the **Borj el Kebir** (also known as Borj Ghazi Mustapha). There has probably been a fort here since Roman times, but the earliest remains are of a fortress built at the end of the 13th century by the Sicilian Roger de Loria. Most of the existing structure dates from the late 15th and early 16th centuries. In 1560 – when controlled by the Spanish – it was the scene of a famous two-month siege and massacre led by the Turkish pirate Dragut, who stormed the castle and killed all its occupants. The skulls of the defeated Spanish soldiers were dumped in an 11m-high pile close to the port; today a small white monument marks the spot.

Among several interesting mosques (all closed to non-Muslims) is the multi-domed Mosque of the Strangers, the Jami'et-Turuk (the Mosque of the Turks) which has a beautiful minaret and the Zaouia de Sidi Brahim which contains the tomb of a 17th-century saint.

The **Musée des Arts et Traditions Populaires** (Museum of Arts and Popular Traditions) is housed in a former mosque – the Zaouia de Sidi Zitouna. Dedicated to Jerban culture, it has a large collection of costumes and jewellery; a reconstruction of a pottery workshop with some huge jars which were used to store everything from grain to clothing; and another room is filled with antique wooden chests.

MIDOUN ✪✪

Jerba's second biggest town really springs into life on Friday – market day – when streets all around the centre are filled with makeshift stalls, attracting a large crowd of local people and tourists. Try to arrive as early as possible, because it is all but over by lunchtime. Another crowd-puller takes place on Tuesday afternoons, when a mock Berber wedding procession, Fantasia, is held for the benefit of visitors.

➕ 28C3
✉ 16km east of Houmt Souq
🍴 Several (£–££)
🚌 Frequent from Houmt Souq and the tourist resorts

SIDI MAHREZ ✪✪

Starting at Flamingo Point about 8km east of Houmt Souq and extending as far as Ras Taguermes (marked by a lighthouse), this 10km stretch of coastline is said to be the best beach in Jerba. The *zone touristique* occupies some of this with its cluster of large hotels, but there are quieter areas. Another unspoilt stretch can be found south of Aghir while the wild and rocky west coast is almost totally uninhabited.

➕ 28C4
✉ 8–18km east of Houmt Souq
🍴 Bar snacks at the beach hotels
🚌 Bus from Houmt Souq

What to See in the South

28A4

60km northwest of Tozeur

No public transport; join an organised excursion or hire a car

Above: *Steep limestone cliffs overlook the palmery at Chebika*

CHEBIKA ✪✪

Chebika is the southernmost of three mountain villages close to the Algerian border which can be visited together on a day trip from Tozeur (►87). The others are Midès (►85) and Tamerza (►86).

Abandoned after serious flooding in 1969, the old village of Chebika is now in ruins, but the villagers are making the most of tourism and still cultivate their gardens. There are guides available to lead you up the mountainside to see the waterfall which feeds the oasis; there is a good view of the salt lake of Chott el Gharsa.

28A3

Kebili is 120km west of Gabès

Small cafés in most oasis towns

Four a day from Gabès

CHOTT EL JERID ✪✪

Chott el Jerid is the most southwesterly of a series of salt lakes lying inland of Gabès (►83). This vast salt lake of shifting colours and mirages covers nearly 5,000sq km. Lifeless in summer, the water evaporates leaving a crust of salt crystals which glisten in the sun, brilliant white interspersed with patches of green, orange and pink, caused by the different chemical constituents of the salts. In winter water collects on either side of the raised causeway built across the Chott from Degache to Kebili (►Drive, 90) and life returns to this inland sea. The lake is fringed with small oasis towns, whose economy depends entirely on the cultivation of dates.

Journeys across the Chott used to be hazardous and all the tourist literature tells of a huge caravan wandering off the main route and disappearing through the thin surface. It's still advised not to go off the beaten track.

Opposite: *Pomegranates ripen in a lush oasis near Gafsa*

DOUZ ✪✪✪

Douz is right on the edge of the desert as most north-erners think of it – the dunes are not quite so impressive here as they are a bit deeper into the Eastern Desert but they are enough for most visitors. Just outside the town near the village of Gleissia is the so-called Great Dune where most tours stop. The town centre is transformed early on a Thursday morning into a frenetic weekly produce market which draws shoppers and traders from a wide area, selling everything from sheep, goats and camels, to dates, spices and beans, as well as clothing and leather goods.

The small but interesting **Douz Museum** explores the history and culture of the southern Jerid with costumes and jewellery, camel harnesses and a Bedouin tent.

GABÈS ✪✪

Initially Gabès appears to be a modern industrial city at the crossroads for tours to the interior, but it has more to offer. It was a major Phoenician and Roman port; during the 14th century it was on the main east–west trading route and was a transit stop for Muslim pilgrims en route to Mecca. It was heavily battered in World War II raids and by devastating floods in 1962 but the old town still has atmosphere with its *souq* and mosques, and its huge plantation of date palms is a true oasis.

GAFSA ✪

A former Berber stronghold and a prosperous Roman town, Gafsa is an important regional centre and phosphate-producing town. Most tourists pass through on their way to the salt lakes and dunes but there is a picturesque *kasbah*, a huge date palm grove and the Piscines Romaines (Roman Pools) with a small museum.

✚ 28B3
✉ 148 km southwest of Gabès
🍴 Choice of cafés (£)
🚌 To Tunis, Tozeur, Sfax, Gabès and Kebili
ℹ Avenue des Martyrs ☎ 75 470351 🕐 Daily 8–6
❓ Annual International Festival of the Sahara, end Dec.
Camel treks organised by Douz Voyages ☎ 75 470178; www.chez.com/douzvoyages; Abdel Moulah Voyages ☎ 75 95484

Douz Museum of the Sahara
✉ Avenue des Martyrs
🕐 Summer: Tue–Sun 7–11, 4–7; winter: 9.30–4.30
🎟 Cheap

✚ 28B4
✉ 405km south of Tunis
🍴 Wide choice of restaurants (£–££)
🚆 To Sfax, Sousse and Tunis
🚌 To Matmata, Tunis, Djerba, Douz, Tataouine
ℹ Place de la Liberté ☎ 75 270254

✚ 28A4
✉ 93km northeast of Tozeur
🍴 Good choice (£–££)
🚌 To Tunis, Tozeur, Sfax
ℹ Place des Piscines Romaines ☎ 76 221664

GORGES DE SELJA ●●

This impressive 15km-long gorge stretches from Redeyef to Metlaoui, a thriving phosphate mining town. One of the best ways to see the gorge is from **Le Lézard Rouge** (the Red Lizard): a restored 19th-century train which operates a two-hour round-trip from Metlaoui. Selja itself is halfway along the gorge and is a good place to stop for a walk down into the deepest parts of the gorge. The railway tunnels and bridges were originally built by the French to transport phosphate from the mines to Gafsa (▶ 83).

KSAR OULED SOLTANE (▶ 22, TOP TEN)

MATMATA ●●●

One of the best-known villages in Tunisia, mostly due to the opening sequence of the original *Star Wars* movie which featured its troglodyte dwellings. Dating from the fourth century BC, many of the underground houses are still inhabited, providing homes that are cool in summer and warm in winter. Some of the houses can be visited by arrangement with the owners, but it is advisable to arrange a price beforehand or buy some of the craft goods on sale. Three of the troglodyte dwellings in Old Matmata have been turned into hotels: the Marhala, part of a chain run by the Touring Club de Tunisie; the Hôtel Sidi Driss whose bar also appeared in the film as the setting for the alien jazz club sequence; and Les Berbères – named after the people who have lived here for centuries.

➕ 28A4
✉ 16km west of Metlaoui
🚂 Le Lézard Rouge
  ✉ Metlaoui station
  ☎ 76 241469; one departure a day
👜 Expensive

Below: *This ancient underground dwelling at Matmata has been converted into a hotel*

➕ 28B3
✉ 43km southwest of Gabès
🚌 Up to ten buses a day to Gabès and daily services to Djerba, Sfax, Sousse and Tunis
ℹ Main square ☎ 75 240114
🍴 Hôtel Marhala ☎ 75 240015, Hôtel Sidi Driss ☎ 75 240005, Hôtel Berbères ☎ 75 240024
👜 By arrangement

A whitewashed mosque stands alone in the desert near Midès

MIDÈS ○○

The oasis village of Midès is in the mountains which border Algeria. Originally a Berber village, Midès became an outpost of the Roman Empire. All but a handful of residents have now left their single room mud brick houses in the original village perched precariously on the sides of the deep gorge, and moved to the new town which has been built on the other side of the palm grove. The oasis itself is, as usual, a place of refuge from the fierce heat of this desert region. The Tunisian government is now helping to restore the old houses as tourist accommodation, and shops that sell local produce and souvenirs to a small but steadily increasing stream of day-trippers.

 28A4

✉ 75km west of Gafsa

🚌 None; join an organised excursion or hire a car

> ### DID YOU KNOW?
>
> Sufism is a devout sect which has been marginalised by Orthodox Islam. Followers seek to achieve a direct relationship with God through spiritual association rather than by learning Koranic texts. They are known for achieving a trance-like state through chanting, dancing and meditation.

NEFTA ○○

The main attractions in Nefta are the Qasr El-Aïn (▶ 24, Top Ten) which is set in a deep basin (the Corbeille or 'basket') below the town, and the other oasis which lies just to the south. But Nefta itself is worth exploring too. The best-preserved of Nefta's Old Town districts is Ouled ech Cherif, where the narrow alleyways are often covered and the walls are decorated with traditional patterns created in the brickwork. There are literally dozens of mosques throughout the old quarters with Sidi M'Khareg in one of the most scenic positions overlooking the oasis.

Nefta is a centre of Sufism – a branch of Islam (▶ above) – and the town has over a hundred shrines (or *marabouts*), that make this city the holiest in Tunisia after Kairouan (▶ 20–1). The Zaouia de Sidi Brahim is the headquarters of an important Sufi order.

 28A4

✉ 25km west of Tozeur

🍴 Hôtel Marhala (£)
   ✉ avenue de l'Environment ☎ 76 430027

🚌 Six a day to Tozeur. Daily services to Kairouan and Sfax

✈ Tozeur–Nefta airport (23km) for flights to Tunis and Jerba

🛈 Avenue Habib Bourguiba ☎ 76 430236

❓ Thursday is market day

QASR EL-AÏN, NEFTA (▶ 24, TOP TEN)

28C2
70km south of Tataouine
Daily from Tataouine
Cafés (£) on place de l'Indépendance

Above: *The mud-brick village of Tamerza is fast dissolving back into the landscape*

28A4
85km west of Gafsa
Tamerza Palace Hotel (££) ☎ 76 453844; fax 76 453722
Two buses a day to Tunis and three a day to Gafsa
Tourist bureau on main road ☎ 76 485288
Daily 8–1, 3–6

28C3
49km south of Medenine
Hôtel Sangho (££)
3km from town on road to Chenini ☎ 75 860102 Fax 75 862177
To Sfax, Sousse, Djerba, Gabès and Tunis.
Festival of the Ksour, Mar

REMADA ✪

Remada, Tunisia's southernmost town beyond which there is nothing but desert, is dominated by the military, due to the proximity of the Libyan border. Centred on a little oasis where the Romans had a small fort, day-to-day life focuses on the shady place de l'Indépendance. Remada's most distinctive sight is on the southern edge of town – a 15-domed mud brick building once used as a slaughterhouse. Borg Bourguiba, 40km southwest of Remada, is where Habib Bourguiba (► 14) was held prisoner for a year in the early 1950s.

TAMERZA ✪✪

Once a Roman military post called Ad Turres, Tamerza later became the seat of a Christian bishop during the Byzantine era. The original village of Tamerza was devastated by catastrophic flooding in 1969 and now lies abandoned. Today visitors walk through its eerily empty streets; it looks strangely beautiful at night when floodlit and viewed from the comfort of the Tamerza Palace Hotel directly opposite. There is a small waterfall and a swimming area known as the Cascades.

TATAOUINE ✪

A good base for exploring the *ksour* or fortified villages (► 22, Top Ten). Tataouine is a Berber word meaning 'springs' and historically there was an important camel market here; there is still a busy market every Monday and Thursday held in and around the central *souq* – one of the best places to buy *kilims* (woven rugs) and pottery. Ksar Megabla, 2km south of the town centre, offers good views of the surrounding area.

Traditional brick designs adorn the entrance to the oasis in Tozeur

Tozeur

The area around Tozeur has been inhabited since at least 8000 BC, sited around an oasis on the northern shore of the great salt lake of Chott el Jerid (►82). The town prospered as a trading post on the route of the great trans-Saharan caravans but today Tozeur is the focal point of Tunisia's ever-expanding desert tourist industry. Until relatively recently Tozeur was merely an overnight stop on desert safaris from the east coast resorts, but it is now an established resort in its own right.

🟨 28A4
✉ 220km west of Gabès; 450km south of Tunis
🍴 Good choice (£–£££) around avenue Bourguiba
🚌 To Tunis, Nefta, Gafsa and Kebili
✈ Regular flights to Tunis, Djerba and Monastir
ℹ Avenue Abdul Kacem Chebbi ☎ 76 454503
❓ Bedouin Festival, Dec

What to See in Tozeur

BELVÉDÈRE ⭐
This rocky outcrop offers panoramic views over the palm grove (►89), the Chott el Jerid (►82) and the Chott el Gharsa. It is a 20-minute walk from the Dar Cheraït (► below); go early in the morning or at sunset, or at night when the site is floodlit.

✉ 3km southwest of the town centre
🕐 Open access
♿ None
🎟 Free

DAR CHERAÏT MUSEUM ⭐⭐
Purpose-built in the style of an upper-class Tunis townhouse, the displays depict scenes from Tunisian life past and present: there is a typical kitchen, a *bey's* bedroom, a wedding scene, a *hammam* and a Bedouin tent. There are displays of costumes, jewellery, ceramics and sacred books; and the work of weavers, cobblers and tailors is also highlighted. A sound-and-light show called 'One Thousand and One Nights' is based (very) loosely on the book of the same name.

✉ Route Touristique
☎ 76 452100
🕐 8am–midnight
♿ None
🎟 Moderate

87

A Walk Around Tozeur

Distance
5km

Time
Half a day allowing for visits

Start/end point
Grand Hôtel de l'Oasis
 28A4
✉ place des Martyrs
☎ 76 452699

Drinks
Cafés (£) on avenue Habib Bourguiba

This walk combines Tozeur's busy central thoroughfare with a glimpse of the palmery.

Start at the Grand Hôtel de l'Oasis and walk up avenue Habib Bourguiba.

Tozeur's main street is a curious mix of sleepy desert town catering for the everyday needs of local people and brash tourist centre with dozens of shops selling carpets, pottery and stuffed camels.

At the tiered pottery bowl landmark turn right for a look around Tozeur's covered market hall. Walk past the slim sandstone minaret of Mosquée El Farkous, turning right at the end of avenue Habib Bourguiba. Continue straight ahead at place des Martyrs. Take the second right towards Mosquée Sidi Abdesallem at the far end. Veer left towards a dome-shaped tiled monument in front of the École Primaire ibn Chabbat and walk down the left-hand side of the school. After 200m, at the end of a concrete wall, turn right following the path through a courtyard to the palmery.

Tozeur's palmery is a lush oasis of greenery

Tozeur's palmery (► 89) covers around 10sq km, has more than 200,000 palm trees and 200 springs.

After two or three minutes' walk, cross a small stream, turn left out of the palmery and then right following a path leading into the médina. Take the third turning right, under a double arch. Note the roofs made of dried palm trunks.

Call in at the Musée des Arts et Traditions Populaires (► 89).

Turn right out of the museum. At the end of the street turn left which leads back to avenue Habib Bourguiba.

MUSÉE DES ARTS ET TRADITIONS POPULAIRES (MUSEUM OF ARTS AND POPULAR TRADITIONS) ✪

This museum illustrates traditional life with costumes, pottery and furniture. One of the most interesting exhibits is a collection of manuscripts describing Tozeur's water system. Originally conceived in the 13th century by the town's *imam* (religious leader) Ibn Chabbat, the distribution network was handed down orally from generation to generation until finally committed to paper in 1911.

☒ Rue de Kairouan
🕐 Summer: 8–noon, 4–7; winter: 8–noon, 3–6. Closed Mon
Ⓜ Cheap

OULED EL HADEF ✪✪✪

Tozeur's Old Town is a web of narrow alleys which have changed little since the 14th century when it was built by the Ouled el Hadef tribe. Its distinctive architecture is considered to be one of the marvels of Islamic art. Unique to Tozeur and neighbouring Nefta (▶ 85), houses are decorated with geometric motifs (also found on local carpets and shawls). The yellowish bricks are handmade from a mix of local sand and clay, soaked in water, shaped in a wooden frame and left to dry in the sun before being baked in a kiln for three days. The bricks provide excellent insulation against the extremes of the desert climate, swelteringly hot in summer and freezing on winter nights.

☒ North and east of the Hôtel Splendid
🍴 Choice of cafés (£)
Ⓜ Free

PALMERY ✪✪✪

Within the oasis at Tozeur are thousands of date palms and hundreds of springs. The Palmery is best viewed from the Belvédère (▶ 87) from a *calèche* (horse-drawn carriage) which you can rent to drive around the 6km loop, or by bicycle. A popular stop on every tourist circuit is the Paradis, a lush tropical garden with a small zoo. One kilometre further is a new project, Chak-Wak, a theme park based on the history of religions.

The minaret of the Mosque El Farkous is built of thousands of tiny bricks

☒ Northeast of the Market Square
🚗 *Calèches* for hire from opposite the Hôtel Karim
🕐 Open access
Ⓜ Free

Paradis
☒ 3km from centre
🕐 Daily 7.30–sunset

Sound and light show
☒ Near Café El-Barka
Ⓜ 76 460310
Ⓜ Expensive (inc dinner)

Chak Wak
☒ Palmery
🕐 Daily 10–6

8

Tozeur to Kebili: the road across the Chott

Distance
186km

Time
Allow five hours including time for lunch and a bathe in the Roman pool

Start/end point
Tozeur
✚ 28A4

Lunch
Hôtel l'Oasis dar Kebili
(££–£££)
✉ Zone Touristique de Kebili
☎ 75 491436

A drive along the causeway across the Chott El Jerid which can produce stunning mirages.

Leave Tozeur heading northeast on the GP3. After 8km drive through the village of Bouhel, turn right and 3km later pass through Degache, which marks the start of the 80km-long / 2m-high causeway across the Chott.

The Chott El Jerid (► 82) is one of a series of giant salt lakes that divide the north of the country from the true desert landscape of the south. There are no significant landmarks en route; however, look out for the abandoned burnt-out shell of a bus and a handful of isolated huts and stalls selling souvenirs. The terrain can appear to change enormously according to the time of year and the brightness of the sunshine. In winter if there has been quite a lot of rain it is not unusual for the water to look pink on one side of the road and green on the other; this is caused by the natural chemicals in the water.

The first signs of life come as you pass through the village of Souk Lahad, which is worth a short stop. You reach Kebili after another 15km.

Kebili was an important slave-trading town until the 19th century but is now simply a regional transport centre. There is a large palm grove, and just outside town – 1km south on the road to Douz – a Roman bathing pool and *hammam* fed by a 3km-deep borehole.

Leave Kebili, returning to Tozeur along the causeway.

The 80km-long causeway across the Chott el Jerid, the largest salt lake in southern Tunisia

Where To...

Above: *Guellala pottery*
Right: *A character in* A Thousand and
One Nights

Tunis & the North

Prices

The restaurants listed in this section have been grouped into three price categories based on a three-course meal per person without drinks.

£   = budget
     (less than 10D)
££   = moderate
     (15–25D)
£££ = expensive
     (over 25D)

Bizerte

Le Bonheur (£)
Grilled meats, fish and seafood at this simple but convivial local restaurant.
✉ 31 rue Thaalbi ☎ 72 431047 ⏰ Lunch, dinner. Closed in Ramadan

L'Eden (££–£££)
Fresh fish and seafood specialities, as well as excellent meat dishes on a flower-adorned terrace.
✉ route de la Corniche ☎ 72 439023 ⏰ Lunch, dinner

Le Petit Mousse (££)
In hotel of the same name (▶ 100). The upstairs dining room offers an excellent French-inspired menu; in summer grilled fish and pizzas are served outside.
✉ route de la Corniche ☎ 72 432185 ⏰ Lunch, dinner

Le Sport Nautique (£££)
Seafront restaurant near town centre. Ideal for a leisurely lunch, with people-watching thrown in.
✉ boulevard Habib Bougatfa ☎ 72 433262 ⏰ Lunch, dinner

Gammarth

L'Olivier (££–£££)
Spacious Mediterranean restaurant with excellent food. Slick service and stylish surroundings.
✉ La Résidence Hotel, Raoued Plage ☎ 71 910101 ⏰ Lunch, dinner

La Goulette

Le Café Vert (££)
The leader among a cluster of fish restaurants. *Poisson Complet* is popular.
✉ 68 avenue Franklin Roosevelt ☎ 71 736156 ⏰ Lunch, dinner

Mamie-Lily (££)
Mamie Lily and her son Jacob receive people in their home with just six tables serving excellent Jewish-Tunisian cuisine.
✉ 14 avenue Pasteur ☎ 71 737633 ⏰ Lunch, dinner. Closed Fri dinner and Sat lunch

Sidi Bou Saïd

Café des Nattes (£)
Allow time to linger and relax while enjoying a coffee at this atmospheric Moorish café overlooking Sidi Bou Saïd's main street.
✉ place Sidi Bou Saïd ⏰ All day

Café Sidi Chabanne (£)
Sit outside sipping the house speciality – mint tea sprinkled with pinenuts – while admiring the view of the Gulf of Tunis.
✉ rue el Hadi Zarrouk ⏰ All day

La Petite Suède (£–££)
This small tea room, where a Swedish family serves really excellent home-made roulades and cakes, is very popular with young Tunisians.
✉ place du 7 Novembre ☎ 71 741843 ⏰ Lunch, dinner

Tabarka

Touta (£–££)
Great shady terrace with view of the port and the fort, and a large choice of fish fresh from the boats.
✉ Porto Corallo ☎ 78 671018 ⏰ Lunch, dinner. Closed during Ramadan

Tunis

Bolero (££)
This eaterie is located in a scruffy alley off rue de

Yougoslavie, but is very popular with local residents. The main choice is between grilled meats and seafood – and there is a good value tourist menu.

✉ **passage el-Guattar** ☎ **71 255928** 🕐 **Lunch, dinner until 9.30. Closed Sun**

Café de Paris (£)
Always busy and a convenient meeting place and people-watching spot. One of the few cafés to serve beer.

✉ **corner of avenue Habib Bourguiba and avenue de Carthage** 🕐 **All day**

Café Plantation (£)
Smiling, customer-friendly staff and a pleasant ambience make this a welcome addition to Tunis's café scene.

✉ **12–14 rue de Marseille** ☎ **71 343565** 🕐 **All day**

Capitole Restaurant (££)
Long-established first-floor restaurant with a particularly good Franco-Tunisian tourist menu.

✉ **60 avenue Habib Bourguiba** ☎ **71 256601** 🕐 **Lunch, dinner**

Chez Nous (££)
Photos of guests such as Edith Piaf and Muhammad Ali line the walls of this intimate French restaurant which offers good *à la carte* and set menus.

✉ **5 rue de Marseille** ☎ **71 253048** 🕐 **Lunch, dinner. Closed Sun and Ramadan**

Chez Slah (££)
Serving International, Tunisian and French cuisine in an agreeable setting. The house speciality is seafood

fresh from the Gulf of Tunis. Alcohol and beer served and good selection of wine. Popular with locals.

✉ **14 Bis rue Pierre de Coubertin** ☎ **71 258888** 🕐 **Lunch, dinner. Closed Mon**

Dar del-Hadj (££)
Tunisian specialities served in the courtyard of an old house in the *médina*. At night very popular with Tunisians. Live performances of Arab-Moorish music.

✉ **17 rue des Tamis, off rue Jemaa Zitouna** ☎ **71 200894** 🕐 **Lunch, dinner. Closed Mon**

Dar El Jeld (£££)
Said to be the best restaurant in Tunis and it certainly has a grand setting in the former mansion of a fabulously wealthy family. It provides superb Tunisian cooking with gracious service and discreet musical accompaniment. Advance booking recommended.

✉ **rue Dar el Jeld** ☎ **71 560916** 🕐 **Lunch, dinner. Closed Sun**

Mahdaoui (£)
Popular eatery with just five or six simple dishes on the menu. The first floor dining room is much quieter.

✉ **rue Jemaa Zitouna, just opposite the Grand Mosque** 🕐 **Mon–Sat 11–4pm. Closed Sun**

La Mamma (£)
Pizzas and pasta as well as a range of Tunisian dishes at this dependable Italian-style restaurant which draws a continual flow of regular customers. Live music at night.

✉ **11 rue de Marseille** ☎ **71 249106** 🕐 **Lunch, dinner**

Grabbing a Sandwich
If you do not feel like having a full meal at lunchtime, drop in at a sandwich bar or pizzeria (both of which can be found all over Tunisia) and ask for a '*cassecroute*'. This is a thick chunk of French bread – usually buttered with fiery *harissa* sauce – then generously filled with lettuce, tomato, egg, tuna, olives and occasionally boiled potatoes or sausage.

Cap Bon

Self-help for Self-caterers

If you are on a self-catering holiday do not expect Tunisian supermarkets to be as well stocked as those in Europe or North America. Many food stores are part of larger shops selling a variety of household goods. The best advice is to shop Tunisian-style and buy food fresh from market stalls.

El Haouaria
L'Épervier (£–££)

Straightforward food at this popular venue busy with tour groups at lunchtime and a local crowd in the evening.

✉ **3 avenue Habib Bourguiba** ☎ **72 297017** ⏱ **Lunch, dinner**

Hammamet
Café Sidi Bou Hdid (£)

Also known as Café des Muriers. An atmospheric domed café which is at its best on warm summer evenings, when customers spill out on to the surrounding ramparts to sip coffee, smoke *chichas* and mull over the events of the day.

✉ **Seafront end of the *médina*** ⏱ **All day**

Le Carrefour (££)

Adjoining a popular bar run by three brothers. Pizza and fish highly recommended.

✉ **avenue des Nations Unies (outside the town centre close to the Hotel Miramar ➤ 102)** ☎ **72 281776** ⏱ **Lunch, dinner**

Chez Achour (££–£££)

Tucked away in a side street, this restaurant is solidly dependable with a strong local following and outside seating in summer. Fish is the house speciality.

✉ **rue Ali Belahouane, off avenue de la République** ☎ **72 280140** ⏱ **Lunch, dinner**

Gelimer Plage (££–£££)

The trendiest restaurant in town with a very contemporary dining hall and a terrace on the beach, serving delicious Mediterranean food. The menu offers several fish and meat carpaccios, and excellent grilled fish.

✉ **Dar Hayet Hotel (➤ 102)** ☎ **21 403430** ⏱ **Daily until 2am**

La Medina (£–££)

Good but predictable tourist menu, and excellent views over the sea and town.

✉ **Next door to Barberousse, on the *médina* wall** ⏱ **Lunch, dinner**

La Pergola (££)

Pleasant location with a large outside terrace awash with greenery. Efficient service and comprehensive menu: soups and salads to grilled meats and fish.

✉ **Centre Commercial, avenue Habib Bourguiba** ☎ **72 280993** ⏱ **Lunch, dinner**

Pomodoro (££–£££)

The style of this restaurant is as discreet as its first floor location. A seriously classy but unstuffy place to eat, with courteous staff and excellent food.

✉ **avenue Habib Bourguiba** ☎ **72 281254** ⏱ **Lunch, dinner**

Restaurant Barberousse (££)

Hugely popular in the summer months with its roof terrace overlooking the *médina*. Both view and food are good value.

✉ **Entrance to the *médina*** ☎ **72 282037** ⏱ **Lunch, dinner**

Restaurant La Brise (£)

With its tiled floor and plastic tablecloths, this is not an ideal choice for dinner, but it is certainly worth considering for lunch, as its food is both wholesome and cheap.

✉ **2 avenue de la République** ☎ **72 280073** ⏱ **Lunch, dinner**

RestoVert (£)
Cosy movie-themed café with walls lined with film posters. Simple food includes salads and sandwiches.

 avenue de la République
🕐 All day

La Scala (£££)
The pasta is excellent at this intimate Italian restaurant themed around the La Scala Opera House in Milan. Book in advance.

✉ off avenue des Nations Unies ☎ 72 280768
🕐 Lunch, dinner. Closed in winter

La Sirene (£–££)
Casual beachfront restaurant/snack bar with shaded terrace. Wide range of food from pizzas and crêpes to grilled fish and *couscous*.

✉ avenue Assad ibn el Fourat close to Hotel Belle Vue
🕐 Lunch, dinner

Les Trois Moutons (££–£££)
One of the best restaurants in town, with excellent meat and fish dishes. Offers an extensive menu and a good value set dinner.

✉ Centre Commercial, avenue Habib Bourguiba ☎ 72 280981
🕐 Lunch, dinner

Kélibia
Anis (£)
Very good value town centre budget restaurant offering Tunisian specialities and pleasant service.

✉ avenue Erriadh ☎ 72 295777 🕐 Lunch, dinner

Le Geoland (££)
Excellent seafood restaurant at very reasonable prices. Friendly service and a seafront terrace.

✉ avenue des Martyrs
🕐 Lunch in summer

Restaurant El-Mansourah (££)
Choose grilled fish and salad with a bottle of the local Muscat de Kélibia, a refreshing medium-dry white wine.

✉ Out beyond Kélibia's fort, at the southern end of Mansourah Beach ☎ 72 296321
🕐 Lunch, dinner

Nabeul
Café Errachida (£)
A welcoming café specialising in mint tea served with tempting sticky cakes.

✉ avenue Habib Thameur (at the junction with avenue Habib Bourguiba) 🕐 All day

Restaurant Bon Kif (££–£££)
Attracts as many local diners as it does tourists; ideal for a long, lazy lunch or dinner. Excellent grilled fish and succulent seafood, matched with quietly efficient service and Tunisian décor.

✉ avenue Marbella (off avenue Habib Thameur) ☎ 72 222783 🕐 Lunch, dinner

Restaurant de l'Olivier (£££)
This restaurant is not cheap, but it offers up-market French cooking in smart surroundings. The wine list includes imported wines as well as some that have been produced locally.

✉ 6 avenue Hedi Chaker ☎ 72 286613 🕐 Lunch, dinner

Time for Tea?
Although mint tea is Tunisia's national drink, standards can vary enormously. Outside the main tourist areas many cafés serve a very sweet lukewarm mixture of gunpowder tea and sugar – often well stewed. For a piping hot glass of freshly brewed mint tea topped with pinenuts it would be hard to better the Café Sidi Chabanne in Sidi Bou Saïd (▶ 92).

Central Tunisia

Rôtisseries and Gargottes

Rôtisseries are the cheapest of Tunisia's restaurants. Aimed at working men, they are easily identified by a rotating spit of roasting chickens at the entrance. This is usually the only food served – accompanied by chips and salad. Gargottes offer a wider range of food including *chorba* (spicy soup), kebabs and *merguez* sausages, but still served in very basic surroundings.

Iles Kerkennah
Cercina (££)
Excellent fish and seafood, and other specialities of the islands are served on a large terrace overlookimg the sea.
✉ Sidi Frej ☎ 74 489953 ⚪ Lunch, dinner

La Sirène (££)
Looks like a glorified beach hut, but serves excellent fresh fish and seafood. Friendly service and good value. In the summer you can sit out on a shaded terrace overlooking the sea and have a beer.
✉ On the beachfront at the end of the road next to Hôtel el-Jazira in Remla ☎ 74 481118 ⚪ Lunch, dinner

Le Kef
Vénus (££)
One of the best restaurants in town, offering good value set price meals and an extensive à la carte choice. One of the few that serve alcohol.
✉ rue Farhat Hached ☎ 78 200355 ⚪ Lunch, dinner. Closed dinner Fri

Mahdia
Café El-Koucha (£)
Behind a beautiful façade on the seafront, are several vaulted rooms, where excellent croissants are served from breakfast, followed by ice-cream and pastries throughout the day, all home-made.
✉ avenue Cap Africa ☎ 73 692268 ⚪ Lunch, dinner

Le Lido (££–£££)
Brightly lit, Le Lido draws a good mix of tourists and locals. Opposite the fishing port, fish *couscous* is a favourite here, as well as grilled fish and seafood.
✉ avenue Farhat Hached ☎ 73 681339 ⚪ Lunch, dinner

Restaurant el-Moez (£)
Popular with local people; fish soup and *kammounia* are among the specialities served here. No alcohol.
✉ In a small side street between Skifa el Kahla and rue des Fatmides ⚪ Lunch, dinner

Monastir
Le Chandelier (££)
Cosy restaurant where again fish is the main thing on the menu, but there are meat dishes as well. Very good food and a large terrace overlooking the yacht harbour.
✉ Marina ☎ 73 462232 ⚪ Lunch, dinner

La Plage (££)
Dine overlooking the sea at this restaurant close to the fishing port; naturally, fresh fish is the speciality of the house.
✉ place du 3 Août ☎ 73 461124 ⚪ Lunch, dinner. Closed Fri

Les Remparts (£–££)
Concentrates on pizzas during the day, but offers a more extensive menu in the evenings. Service is a little slow, but if you are sitting outside watching the world go by it does not matter too much.
✉ avenue Habib Bourguiba ☎ 73 460752 ⚪ Lunch, dinner

Port El Kantaoui
La Daurade (££–£££)
Fresh fish tops the menu at this popular venue with outdoor seating in demand at

lunch and dinner. Worth booking ahead to secure one of the best tables.

✉ The Marina ☎ 73 244893
🕐 Lunch, dinner

Sfax

El Barreka (£)

This is the reastuarnt you dream of finding on the Mediterranean. A huge wooden hut on stilts in the middle of a beach. The simple food is delicious.

✉ route de Sidi-Mansour, 4.5km north of town 🕐 Daily 8–8 May–Sep

Café Diwan (£)

A popular café with a rooftop terrace offering views over the city wall. A quiet, relaxed place to stop for tea or coffee during the day or to mingle with local people in the evenings. Folklore show Fri 5–7pm.

✉ off rue de la Kasbah, next to No 37 🕐 8 till late

Chez Nous (££)

The food here is good, even if the service is somewhat surly. Tunisian specialities include various *ojjas* (egg dishes) and fish *couscous*.

✉ 26 rue Patrice Lumumba ☎ 74 227128 🕐 Lunch, dinner

Le Corail (£££)

Rather formal but no complaints about the food.

✉ 39 rue Habib Mazoun ☎ 74 210317 🕐 Lunch, dinner

Le Printemps (££)

Smart restaurant serving really good French cuisine.

✉ 55 avenue Habib Bourguiba ☎ 74 226973 🕐 Lunch, dinner

Sousse

La Calèche (£££)

Aimed squarely at the tourist market but most dishes are quite pricey. Excellent set menu is good value.

✉ rue Remada ☎ 73 226489
🕐 Lunch, dinner

Hong Kong Restaurant (£££)

Here is an alternative to *briks* and *couscous* but the *à la carte* selection is quite expensive. The set menu is better value.

✉ boulevard de Rabat – opposite El Hana Beach Hotel ☎ 73 221366 🕐 Lunch, dinner

Le Lido (££)

A restaurant in a great location opposite the port, offering some outside seating. The menu is dominated by excellent fresh fish.

✉ avenue Mohammed V ☎ 73 225329 🕐 Lunch, dinner

Restaurant Le Viking (£££)

Centrally placed off avenue Bourguiba, Le Viking can be expensive so it's best to stick to the set menus.

✉ rue de l'Algerie ☎ 73 228377 🕐 Lunch, dinner

Tip Top (££)

Aimed at the holiday market but also attracting Tunisians, Tip Top is a deservedly popular choice, offering a warm welcome, cosy ambience in a restored Turkish house and excellent choice of food.

✉ boulevard de la Corniche ☎ 73 226158 🕐 Lunch, dinner

Blowing Bubbles

In most bars there will be several men smoking *chichas* – also known as hookah pipes. This is the most popular way of smoking in Tunisia. Contrary to popular perception, the water pipes are not filled with hashish but with *tombac*, a close relative of tobacco. The *tombac* is placed on top of the pipe and covered with a very hot piece of charcoal. The smoke is then filtered through the water before being inhaled.

Jerba & the South

Tipping and TGV

Waiters do not expect to be tipped in the same way as they do in Europe and North America. In budget restaurants it is acceptable to leave a few coins unless the food and service were exceptional, in which case you may wish to leave more. In tourist restaurants it is more normal to leave ten per cent – but only if the service merits it. Always check to see if service has already been included. TGV is not the service charge but a sales tax.

Gabès

Restaurant de l'Oasis (£££)

Generally reckoned to be the top spot in Gabès. The set menu is good value.

✉ **17 avenue Farhat Hached** ☎ **75 270098** 🕐 **Lunch, dinner**

Restaurant du Port (£–££)

There is no sign for this place but everyone knows it. The best grilled fish, octopus salad and fish couscous.

✉ **avenue Hedi Chaker** 🕐 **Lunch, dinner until 9pm**

Jerba

Aladin (£)

Fish and some interesting seafood dishes at this small, low-priced restaurant.

✉ **40 avenue Mohamed Badra, Houmt Souq** 🕐 **Lunch, dinner**

Dar Faïza (£)

Good value set price menu in a cosy hotel dining room where it can be hard to find a table in high season.

✉ **rue de la République, Houmt Souq** ☎ **75 650083; fax 05 651763** 🕐 **Dinner**

El Foundouk (££)

Intimate and cosy restaurant in the shade of an old tree. Very good Tunisian specialities.

✉ **avenue Habib Bourguiba, Houmt Souq** ☎ **75 653238** 🕐 **Lunch, dinner**

La Fontaine (£)

In summer this is a good place for home-made ice-creams, otherwise snacks, drinks and pizzas are served on a shaded terrace.

✉ **rue du 2 Mars, Houmt Souq, opposite Mosque of the Turks** 🕐 **Daily**

E-Guestile (£–££)

Rather elegant restaurant decorated with old objects. Very good Tunisian dishes.

✉ **21 rue Marsa Ettefa, Midoun** 🕐 **Lunch, dinner**

El Hana (££–£££)

Dine by candlelight with linen napkins and tablecloths at this snug, welcoming little restaurant which feels like someone's front room. The food is very good with exceptional mashed potato dishes.

✉ **place Mohamed Ali, Houmt Souq** ☎ **75 650568** 🕐 **Dinner**

La Mamma (£)

You can eat with the locals at this atmospheric and cheap eatery which does a roaring trade in soups and *couscous*.

✉ **rue Habib Bourguiba, Houmt Souq** 🕐 **All day**

Les Palmiers (£)

Come to this friendly restaurant for great value eating. With its colourful menu, pretty tablecloths, pictures on the wall and subtle lighting it is a cut above most Tunisian budget restaurants and worth a visit. No alcohol is permitted.

✉ **place d'Algerie, Houmt Souq** 🕐 **Lunch, dinner**

La Princesse d'Haroun (£££)

Jerba's most famous restaurant. In summer you can eat on the terrace overlooking the harbour. Meat dishes available but seafood starters and grilled fish rule the waves. Smart casual dress preferred.

✉ Opposite the fishing harbour ☎ 75 650488
🕐 Lunch, dinner

Restaurant du Sportif (£–££)
Starkly lit restaurant catering for a mainly local clientele. The menu consists of mostly with meat grills and stews.
✉ 147 avenue Habib Bourguiba 🕐 11–9

Tamerza
Tamerza Palace Hotel (££)
Good for lunch or dinner with agreeable food, attentive service and excellent views of the abandoned village of Tamerza.
✉ Tamerza ☎ 76 485322; fax 76 485322 🕐 Lunch, dinner

Tozeur
Al-Qods (£)
Extremely popular café-patisserie with the best sweets and pastries in town. Very good Tunisian sandwiches at lunch.
✉ avenue Habib Bourguiba, in front of the mosque 🕐 Daily 6am–10pm

Les Andalous (££)
One of the only restaurants that serves specialities from Tozeur (order 24-hours in advance).
✉ Hotel du Jardin, boulevard de l'Environnement, road to Degache ☎ 76 454196 🕐 Lunch, dinner

La Diamanta (£)
This is a good family-run restaurant, which serves classic French and Tunisian dishes.
✉ avenue Abou El Kacem Chabbi ☎ 76 453867 🕐 Lunch, dinner

Le Palmeraie (£££)
An expensive but pleasant hotel restaurant offering high standards of food and service. A tourist menu is available.
✉ Hotel Palmeraie ☎ 76 452041 🕐 Lunch, dinner

Le Petit Prince (££)
Long-established restaurant which sometimes has evening shows of traditional music and dancing.
✉ off avenue Abou el Kacem Chabbi leading into the palmery ☎ 76 452518 🕐 Dinner

Restaurant de la République (£)
Tucked away in a corner, this cosy little restaurant appeals to local people and tourists. Good, affordable food.
✉ avenue Habib Bourguiba (on the west side at the back of an arcade of shops) 🕐 Lunch, dinner

Restaurant du Sud (£)
Basic restaurant very popular with young travellers, serving a range of Tunisian specialities at rock bottom prices.
✉ avenue Farhat Hached (opposite Agil petrol station) ☎ 76 450826 🕐 Lunch, dinner

Le Soleil (£)
Opposite Résidence Warda, the best of Tozeur's budget options with clean surroundings and an extensive menu. Camel-meat *couscous* is available if ordered in advance.
✉ avenue Abou Kacem el Chabbi ☎ 76 554220 🕐 Lunch, dinner

Hot-Headed
Harissa can be a bit of a shock to the system on first acquaintance but many visitors develop such a liking for the fiery hot chilli paste that they take home a jar or two at the end of their trip. Used throughout the countries of the Maghreb for soups, stews and *couscous*, it is made up from ground dried red chilli peppers, garlic, coriander, cumin seeds, sea salt and olive oil.

Tunis & the North

Prices

The hotels listed are grouped into three categories based on one night's double room in high season including breakfast and taxes. All rooms have en-suite facilities unless otherwise stated.

£ = budget (under 30D)

££ = moderate (30D–80D)

£££ = expensive (over 80D)

Bizerte
Bizerta Resort (£££)
Beachfront hotel in the *Zone Touristique* with indoor and outdoor swimming pools and a health club. The bedrooms are equipped with minibars and satellite television.

✉ **route de la Corniche** ☎ **72 436966; fax 72 422955**

Le Petit Mousse (££)
Well-run hotel with an excellent restaurant (➤ 92). One of its few negative features is that the private beach is just a very narrow strip, close to the road.

✉ **route de la Corniche, 6km from the centre** ☎ **72 432185; fax 72 437595**

Gammarth
La Résidence (£££)
One of Tunisia's newest and most luxurious hotels with a thalassotherapy spa, tennis courts, Mediterranean restaurant and free shuttle service to Tunis city centre.

✉ **2km north of Gammarth** ☎ **71 910101; fax 71 749888**

Sidi Bou Saïd
Dar Said (££–£££)
Delightful hotel in a restored 19th-century house in the heart of Sidi Bou Said, set around four patios with fountains, fragrant with jasmine and bougainvillea. There is a small swimming pool in the peaceful garden with century-old cypress trees overlooking the sea.

✉ **rue Toumi** ☎ **71 729666; www.darsaid.com.tn**

Sidi-Bou-Farès (£)
This picturesque old house contains ten comfortable rooms, set around a courtyard covered in hibiscus and bougainvillea, and with a fig tree.

✉ **Take the stairway left at the Café des Nattes** ☎ **71 740091**

Sidi Bou Saïd (£££)
This small renovated hotel is owned by the Tunisian National Tourist Office to provide hands-on experience for students at the adjacent hotel school. Full of character, it has a swimming pool, tennis courts and – from its sun terrace – an excellent view of Tunis.

✉ **avenue Sidi Dhrif (800m north of the village)** ☎ **71 740411; fax 71 745129**

Tabarka
Abou Nawas Montazah (£££)
This sprawling beachfront hotel boasts tennis courts and a diving centre – but the rooms can be very noisy.

✉ **route Touristique** ☎ **78 673532; fax 78 673530**

Les Aiguilles (££)
Small hotel in the centre with comfortable rooms. Those on the third floor have access to a balcony.

✉ **18 avenue Bourguiba** ☎ **78 673789**

Les Mimosas (££)
Moorish-style hotel in an old palace on a hill, with fantastic views.

✉ **On the road above the petrol station at the entrance to town** ☎ **78 673018; www.hotel-les-mimosas.com**

Robinson Club Tabarka (£££)
Luxurious resort hotel with thalassotherapy centre, water sports and pools.

✉ **route Touristique, 4km out of town** ☎ **78 670000; www.robinson-tunisia.com**

Tunis

Abou Nawas (£££)

Located next to the Palais du Congres and within walking distance of the *médina*, this is one of Tunis's top hotels. It houses a high-class Italian restaurant, a fitness centre and a pool.

✉ **avenue Mohamed V** ☎ **71 350355; fax 71 352882**

Africa (£££)

One of the city's major landmarks and meeting points (► 30), Africa is conveniently situated fronting the bustling main thoroughfare, a ten-minute walk from the *médina*. The hotel's facilities are more modern than its drab, ugly exterior might suggest.

✉ **50 avenue Habib Bourguiba** ☎ **71 347477;** **www.elmouradi.com**

Carlton (££)

A clean, central mid-market hotel, but lacking in warmth both in its rooms and the attitude of the staff.

✉ **31 avenue Habib Bourguiba** ☎ **71 330644;** **www.carltontunis.com**

Dar el Medina (££–£££)

The first hotel in the *médina* in a fabulous, grand old house, run by the Belahouen family who lived here in style until 2003, when they turned it into a luxury hotel. The decoration and eye for detail is wonderful, and kept totally in line with traditional *médina* architecture.

✉ **64 rue Sidi ben Arous** ☎ **71 563022;** **www.darelmedina.com**

Excel (££)

A centrally located, clean and comfortable hotel, offering in-room television and telephone and a friendly bar.

✉ **35 avenue Habib Bourguiba** ☎ **71 355129;** **www.hotelexcel.com**

Hotel de Russie (£££)

Spotless hotel with typically Tunisian-style rooms discreetly located in a back street just off the bustling rue el Jazira.

✉ **18 rue de Russie** ☎ **71 328883; fax 71 321685**

Maison Dorée (£–££)

A well-maintained budget hotel with good bedding and the atmosphere of a bygone age. The staff are a little formal and unless you particularly like the sound of trams thundering past your window every few minutes ask for a room at the front of the hotel.

✉ **6 rue de Hollande (entrance in rue el Koufa)** ☎ **71 240631; fax 71 332401**

Majestic (££)

One of the great old-established hotels of Tunis, now showing its age.

✉ **36 avenue de Paris** ☎ **71 332848;** **www.majestichotel.com.tn**

Médina (£)

Probably the most pleasant of the Old Town budget hotels with clean double rooms; there are no singles or en-suite facilities.

✉ **place de la Victoire** ☎ **71 327497**

Transatlantique (£)

Another fairly basic hotel with large and noisy bedrooms, but attractively tiled lobby and passageways.

✉ **106 rue de Yougoslavie** ☎ **71 334319**

Bargain Beds

Outside the peak summer months the price of beds comes right down, often to half the high season rate. Hotel prices are fixed by the Ministry of Tourism and are usually displayed in hotel reception areas. Always agree on the rate in advance and ask to see the room before making up your mind.

Cap Bon

Tourist Terrain

Tunisia is very fond of its *zone touristiques* (tourist areas) where most big holiday hotels are located. They are often sited along some of the best stretches of beach, but they are usually also several kilometres from the heart of a town and so lack local flavour. They also give the impression that the Tunisian authorities want to keep tourists and local people apart – which rather defeats the object of visiting someone else's country.

Hammamet

Aziza (£££)

A family-oriented beachfront hotel which is very popular with tour groups. It includes a health club, tennis courts and disco.

✉ **boulevard Assad ibn el Fourat (3km from town centre)**
☎ **72 283666; fax 72 283099**

Bel Azur (£££)

A Moorish-style hotel on a small headland with pretty gardens and two sandy beaches. There is a separate children's pool as well as a pizzeria, snack bar and an *à la carte* restaurant.

✉ **avenue Assad ibn el Fourat (2km from town centre)** ☎ **72 280544; fax 72 280275**

Belle Vue (£)

The advantage of this hotel is its superb beachfront location just 400m from the *médina*, but the rooms are looking dilapidated now.

✉ **avenue Assad ibn el Fourat**
☎ **72 281121; email: kaismohdi@yahoo.com**

Dar Hayet (££–£££)

The smallest and most discreet of Hammamet's deluxe hotels. Rooms are all doubles and are plushly decorated with locally produced furnishings; most have sea views.
There is a pool, and a small café.

✉ **rue de la Corniche** ☎ **72 282856; fax 72 283399**

Hasdrubal (£££)

Hammamet's top hotel, with all facilities and extremely luxurious rooms and surroundings.

✉ **South end of Hammamet Yasmine** ☎ **72 248800; www.lhw.com**

Khella (££)

Town centre hotel within two minutes' walk of several restaurants. Comfortable and clean with cosy rooms.

✉ **avenue de la République**
☎ **72 283900; fax 72 283704**

La Maison de Claudine (£–££)

The hotel is well maintained and sits on a pleasantly uncrowded strip of beach. Shops and restaurants just across the road.

✉ **route Touristique South, 4km from the centre**
☎ **72 281564; email: noe@topnet.tn**

Le Mirage (£–££)

Very clean rooms in a modern building, and a helpful French owner who is incredibly knowledgeable about the region. Wonderful terrace with a view over the town and the beach.

✉ **173 avenue de la République** ☎ **72 280601**

Miramar (£££)

The hotel is well maintained and sits on a pleasantly uncrowded strip of beach. Shops and restaurants just across the road.

✉ **rue des Hôtels (4km from the centre)**
☎ **72 280344; email: miramar.hammamet@planet.tn**

Les Orangers (£££)

This two-hotel complex is some way out of the town centre. It offers a sandy beach, colourful gardens, a health club and a regular programme of evening entertainment. Perfect for families.

✉ **rue des Hôtels**
☎ **72 280144; www.tunisia-orangers.com**

Residence Hammamet (£–££)

One of Hammamet's longest-established tourist hotels and still one of the best. All rooms sleep up to four and have mini-kitchens. There is a rooftop terrace with swimming pool and a private beach; very close to the *médina*.

✉ **60 avenue Habib Bourguiba**
☎ **72 280406; fax 72 280396**

Shératon (£££)

An extensive resort hotel with rooms built in small clusters in lush gardens. There are six tennis courts, a swimming pool and children's play area.

✉ **route Touristique Hammamet Sud (6km from town centre)** ☎ **72 226555; email: reservations_hammamet_tunisia@sheraton.com**

El Haouaria
L'Épervier (££)

Situated off the main street and built round a pretty courtyard with jasmine and orange trees. A clean and comfortable hotel with almost the only restaurant in town.

✉ **avenue Habib Bourguiba**
☎ **72 297017; fax 72 297258**

Kélibia
Palmarina (££)

Newish hotel with swimming pool, café/bar and restaurant. The sun terrace overlooks a small beach and the colourful fishing harbour. Friendly, helpful staff.

✉ **avenue des Martyrs** ☎ **72 274062; fax 72 274055**

Nabeul
Le Fakir (£–££)

Family-run hotel in a quiet residential era. Impeccable and spacious rooms with bathrooms, and some with a terrace and views over the sea.

✉ **Route touristique**
☎ **72 285477**

Hôtel Lido (£££)

A large complex with cottages in the grounds as well as the main hotel building. Every facility you would expect from a popular package destination.

✉ **3km east of Nabeul**
☎ **72 362988; email: h.lido@planet.tn**

Les Jasmins (££)

In a secluded tree-lined road five minutes' walk from a quiet beach. Popular with tour groups in summer, independent guests are still welcomed. Rooms are in two-storey blocks in gardens. Swimming pool and up-market seafood restaurant.

✉ **rue Abou el Kacem Chabbi (just outside Nabeul town centre)** ☎ **72 285343; email: hotel.jasmins@gnet.tn**

Pension Les Oliviers (£–££)

A cut above average guesthouse with clean rooms and en-suite bathrooms in a large modern house surrounded by olive and citrus trees. Close to the beach and a minute's walk from the Hôtel Les Jasmins (► above).

✉ **11 rue Abou el-Kacem Chabbi** ☎ **72 286865; email: pensionlesoliviers@yahoo.com**

Don't be Star-Struck

Do not pay too much attention to hotel star ratings as they can be very unreliable. Introduced some years ago, the star system was only ever intended to grade the physical facilities of a hotel – ignoring the quality of service offered altogether. Now, even the assessing of facilities seems somewhat lax.

Central Tunisia

Food for Thought

Avoid beach resort hotels which insist that you book half- or full-board. Hotels find this a useful way to boost their income, but for guests it can mean an endless round of rather bland 'international-style' buffets. It is far more interesting and adventurous to eat out – and frequently cheaper as well.

Iles Kerkennah

Cercina (£–££)
Comfortable rooms – most are literally on the beach. The very friendly owner, Chokri, does his best to make his guests to feel at home. Great terrace.
✉ Sidi Frej ☎ 74 489953; email: hotel.Cercina@planet.tn

Grand (££)
Secluded beachfront hotel with spacious rooms, a swimming pool and tennis courts. Cycling and horse-riding available nearby.
✉ Sidi Frej ☎ 74 489861; email: seabel@grand-hotel-kerkennah.com.tn

Jazira (£)
Small family-run hotel in the Old Town district of Mahdia.
✉ Er Remla ☎ 74 481145

Kairouan

Al-Kasbah (££)
Built like a kasbah, but in fact modern, this is the best hotel in Kairouan with a great pool in the courtyard.
✉ avenue Ibn el-Jazzar ☎ 77 237301

Splendid (££)
Probably Kairouan's classiest hotel – although it has seen better days. The big rooms are clean and comfortable and have private bathrooms. Bar and licensed restaurant.
✉ rue 9 April (off avenue de la République) ☎ 77 227522 Fax 77 230829

Mahdia

Cap Mahdia (££)
A bit far from the centre, but beautiful Moorish architecture and comfortable rooms with sea views.
✉ route Touristique ☎ 73 680300; email: capmahdia@abounawas.com.tn
🚫 Closed Nov–Mid-Mar

Corniche (£)
Good value, small modern hotel about 2km west of the town centre.
✉ avenue 7 Novembre (just before Zone Touristique) ☎ 73 694201; fax 73 692196

Monastir

Yasmine (£–££)
Family-run pension with single and double rooms and a licensed restaurant.
✉ route de la Falaise ☎ 73 501546

Port El Kantaoui

El Hana Hannibal Palace (£££)
One of Port El Kantaoui's longest-established hotels just a short stroll from the marina. Pleasant ambience with a popular lunchtime terrace restaurant.
☎ 73 348577; fax 73 348321

Sfax

Abou Nawas (£££)
This well-located hotel, mainly aimed at business travellers, could do with sharpening up all round, from its dreary décor to its sluggish service.
✉ avenue Habib Bourguiba ☎ 74 225700; email: sfax@abounawas.com.tn

Alexandre (£)
Very good value at this elegant old colonial-style building with enormous baths.
✉ 21 rue Alexandre Dumas ☎ 74 221613

La Paix (£)
Fairly basic hotel. Although rooms have showers, you have to be a bit of a

contortionist to use them.
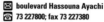 **17 rue Alexandre Dumas**
☎ **74 296437**

Sousse
Abou Nawas Boujafaar (£££)
A mix of business travellers and holidaymakers at this plush beachfront hotel which is equally well placed for shopping and eating out. Facilities include a couple of popular bars, a terrace restaurant and a thalassotherapy spa.
✉ **avenue Habib Bourguiba**
☎ **73 22603;**
www.abounawas.com.tn

Claridge (£)
Once the most superior place in town, now overshadowed by the string of beach hotels along the corniche. Plenty of character and a central location between the *médina* and the beach. The large comfortable rooms all have a bath or shower – but not all have en-suite toilets.
✉ **10 avenue Habib Bourguiba**
☎ **73 224759; fax 73 227277**

Emira
Atmospheric *médina* hotel. All rooms have bath or shower and toilet. Staff are friendly and helpful. Breakfast is served on a rooftop terrace.
✉ **52 rue de France** ☎ **73 226325**

El Hana Beach (£££)
A popular family hotel in colourful gardens. Guests can use the facilities of two neighbouring hotels: the El Hana and the Chems El Hana.
✉ **boulevard de la Corniche**
☎ **73 226900; fax 73 226076**

Farès (££)
Busy city centre hotel next to the railway station. All rooms have bathrooms and balconies.
✉ **boulevard Hassouna Ayachi**
☎ **73 227800; fax 73 227380**

Hadrumète (£–££)
A once-flourishing two-star hotel which has fallen behind the times. Close to the port, it still retains plenty of character. Ask for a room with a balcony and enjoy the hotel's faded glory.
✉ **place Assad ibn el Fourat**
☎ **73 226291; fax 73 226863**

Médina (£)
One of the best hotels in the *médina*. Rooms have en-suite bathrooms and open on to a small courtyard.
✉ **15 rue Othman Osman**
☎ **73 221722**

Paris (£)
Beautifully maintained budget hotel just inside the walls of the *médina*. Friendly management, lots of atmosphere – but shared washing facilities!
✉ **15 rue Rempart Nord** ☎ **73 220564; fax 73 219038**

Sousse Azur (££)
Friendly, comfortable, close to the beach and good value for money.
✉ **5 rue Amilcar** ☎ **73 227760**

Tej Mahaba (£££)
A massive 700-bed hotel, 200m from the beach in large gardens with indoor and outdoor pools, tennis courts, Turkish bath and seafood restaurant.
✉ **avenue Taieb Mehiri**
☎ **73 229800;**
www.marhababeach.com

Women Travellers
Finding somewhere to stay presents extra problems for women travellers, whether holidaying alone or in pairs. Cultural differences mean that western women can face a certain amount of pestering although serious threats are rare. The best advice is generally to avoid small *médina* hotels and stay in family-run pensions or major tourist hotels instead.

Jerba & the South

Marhalas

The Touring Club de Tunisie runs a chain of cheap, traditional hotels known as *marhalas*. Priced slightly higher than youth hostels, they offer basic but clean rooms and a warm welcome. The most popular *marhalas* include the one in Houmt Souq and the underground hotel at Matmata.

Douz

El Medina (£)

Pleasant hotel with an Arab-style café and a large roof terrace with good views. Clean and comfortable rooms, the only drawback is the mandatory wake-up call from the mosque opposite.
✉ rue el-Hanine, near place du Marché ☎ 75 470010

Mouradi (££)

Indoor and outdoor pools, a gym and *hammam* at this newest of the *Zone Touristique* hotels.
✉ Zone Touristique ☎ 75 470303; fax 75 470905

Sun Palm Hotel (££)

Atmospheric mid-market hotel attracting a mix of Tunisians and tourists. Rooms are comfortable if rather sparse and service is very casual.
☎ 75 470123;
www.goldenyasmin.com

Gabès

Atlantic (£)

Once-grand colonial-style hotel long past its best, but still with some character.
✉ 4 avenue Habib Bourguiba ☎ 75 220034; fax 75 221358

Chems (££)

Enormous beachfront bungalow complex with single and double rooms.
✉ On the beach
☎ 75 270547;
www.hotelchems.com.tn

Jerba

Dar Faïza (££)

Simple but comfortable hotel set in the old villa of a French count, just outside the centre of Houmt Souk. The rooms overlook the lush bougainvillea gardens with a swimming pool.
✉ 6 rue de la République, opposite the Borj el-Kebir
☎ 75 650083;
www.darfaizadarsalem.com

Djerba Midoun (£–££)

Very well kept small hotel with comfortable rooms around a pleasant courtyard.
✉ rue de 13 Aout, Midoun
☎ 75 730006

Erriadh (£)

This delightful *fondouk* (► panel, 107) in the heart of Houmt Souq oozes charm and character. Built around a vine-covered courtyard, rooms are prettily tiled and have en-suite facilities.
✉ 10 rue Mohamed Ferjani
☎ 75 650756; email: moumirherbegue@gnet.tn

Lotos (£–££)

Very spacious rooms, many with large balconies overlooking the coast.
✉ 18 rue de la République
☎ 75 650026; fax 75 650127

Marhala (£)

One of several character budget hotels run by the Touring Club de Tunisie (► panel). Small and basic rooms but loads of atmosphere and a busy bar.
✉ 13 rue Moncef Bey ☎ 75 650146; fax 75 653317

Sables d'Or (£)

Converted house with a central patio in the centre of Houmt Souq. The 12 rooms are kept spotlessly clean and all have showers – but there are communal toilets.
✉ 30 rue Mohammed Ferjani
☎ 75 650423

Ulysse Palace (£££)

Beachfront hotel with

several restaurants, a thalassotherapy spa; minibars and satellite television in rooms.

✉ Zone Touristique ☎ 75 758777 ; www.movenpick-djerba.com

Matmata
Marhala (£)

This converted underground house is run by the Touring Club de Tunisie (▶ panel). Popular, so book well ahead.

✉ off Toujane road ☎ 75 240015

Nefta
Marhala (£-££)

This former brick factory on the edge of Nefta's oasis is now a hotel run by the Touring Club de Tunisie. Comfortable and friendly, it has recently opened a new wing and swimming pool.

✉ route Touristique ☎ 76 430027; email: marhala@yahoo.fr

Rose (£££)

Block-booked by mainly German tour groups in the peak summer season, this comfortable hotel is often almost empty in winter when room rates take a dramatic dive. Big pool in summer.

✉ route Touristique ☎ 76 430697; fax 76 430385

Sahara Palace (££#)

The most luxurious hotel in the oasis, favoured by French movie stars, with the largest pool, and great views over the oasis.

✉ route de la Corbeille ☎ 76 432048; www.saharapalace.com.tn

Tamerza
Tamerza Palace Hotel (££–£££)

Stylish, well-run hotel overlooking the ruined village of Tamerza. A good base for exploring the desert region.

☎ 76 453722; fax 76 799910

Tozeur
Abou Nawas (£££)

Palatial hotel on the edge of the palm grove with an elegant marble-floored lobby with gushing fountain. Bedrooms are in two-storey blocks in the gardens. French speciality restaurant or a gloomy cafeteria.

✉ route Touristique ☎ 76 453500; www.abounawas.com.tn

Basma (£££)

Laid-back tourist hotel very popular with French tour groups. Attractive bar and lobby area. Dull bedrooms.

✉ route Touristique ☎ 76 452488; email: hotel.basma@gnet.tn

Continental (££)

Long-established mid-market hotel on the edge of the palm grove with comfortable rooms and a swimming pool.

✉ avenue Aboul Kacem Chebbi ☎ 76 461526

Grand Hotel de L'Oasis (££)

Popular with tourists on desert safaris. The rooms are a bit like cells but the service is friendly and there is a decent bar and restaurant.

✉ avenue Aboul Kacem Chebbi ☎ 76 452699; fax 76 452153

Résidence Warda (£)

Simple but pleasant rooms with en-suite showers and scorching hot water. Lovely roof terrace.

✉ avenue Abdel Kacem Chebbi ☎ 76 452597

Fondouks

Similar to *marhalas* in offering simple accommodation at cheap prices, *fondouk* hotels – of which there are several in Jerba – have all been built round old courtyards. Originally these would have been used for stabling horses and storing goods while merchants lived in rooms above. *Fondouk* hotels are some of the most atmospheric in Tunisia and well worth a night or two's stay.

Shopping in Tunisia

Hassle...

Do not expect to be allowed to shop in peace in Tunisia. There is little understanding – or desire to understand – the concept of browsing. Enter a tourist shop and an 'assistant' will immediately shadow your every move continuously pointing out the obvious, informing you very graciously that there is 'no charge for looking' and seizing upon even a slight flicker of interest in any item.

Markets

No trip to Tunisia would be complete without at least one visit to a local market. Outside the main towns they are the driving force and economic hub of rural communities. Lives are planned around the event: it is not only where all purchases are made for the week ahead but is a chance to see friends and catch up on local gossip. Tunisian markets are noisy, bustling and colourful and – even if you are not planning to buy anything – they have a wonderful atmosphere, are great for photographs and provide a fascinating insight into the Tunisian way of life.

Market Days

Monday: El Jem, Kairouan, Matmata, Houmt Souk
Tuesday: Kebili
Wednesday: Menzel Bourguiba, Gafsa
Thursday: Douz, Le Kef, Nefta, Hammamet
Friday: Nabeul, Tabarka, El Haouaria, Mahdia, Sfax, Midoun
Saturday: Monastir
Sunday: Sousse, Tozeur

Carpets

Carpet-making is one of Tunisia's most traditional crafts dating from as early as the 14th century. While not cheap, they make a handsome and long-lasting souvenir and are readily available all over Tunisia particularly in Tunis, El Jem, Sfax and, of course, Kairouan – the King of the Carpet Centres. Make sure any carpet you purchase has a label of authenticity attached.

The most expensive carpets are knotted, and are priced according to the number of knots per square metre. As a general rule, the firmer the pile and the sharper the definition of the pattern, the greater the value of the carpet and the longer it will last. You can also purchase the woven carpets known as kilims, which usually feature traditional Berber motifs – these are reasonably cheap to buy.

Pottery

Cheap, colourful and very collectible, Tunisian pottery makes the ideal souvenir. Nabeul and Guellala on the island of Jerba are the two big production centres although pottery is sold all over the country. Nabeul's industry dates back to Roman times with many of today's most popular designs and colours (blue and white, and yellow and green) the same as those used 2,000 years ago. Best buys include plates, bowls, vases and tiles which – if you buy several – can make a very attractive wall panel.

Jewellery

Almost every *souq* in the country has its jewellery section. Most Tunisian gold is only 12 or 14 carat while silverwork is often *metal argente* (silver plating). Houmt Souq in Jerba is one of the best places for silver and gold pieces. Common motifs include fishes and the Hand of Fatima, Islam's principal female cult figure who was the daughter of the Prophet Mohammed. The Berber regions of the south specialise in chunky silver jewellery often set with semi-precious stones. In Tabarka you will find a lot of coral jewellery – but since coral is endangered and protected, it has probably been gathered illegally.

Woodwork and Metalwork

The best wood carving is to be found in Sfax where olive wood is turned into bowls, spoons and chess boards. The tapping of hammers and chisels on brass is a familiar sound in any of the *souqs* where ashtrays, plates and trays are among the most popular items. Craftsman will often offer to engrave a name on pieces bought.

Clothes

Traditional clothes like the *burnous* (a heavy woollen coat) and *chechias* (the traditional red felt hat still worn by many men) can be tempting, but will it ever be worn back at home! All the *souqs* sell this kind of item.

Kitchenware and food

If you like couscous, bring back a *couscoussier*, which is also handy to steam vegetables. Mint tea is good for you, so look for the inexpensive blue teapots. Sahel olive oil and olives are excellent, as is the Tunisian harissa (chilli sauce). No one will refuse the delicious marzipan sweets available from Tunisian pâtisseries..

Stuffed camels and bird cages

Lined up in rows outside dozens of souvenir shops – particularly in Port El Kantaoui and Hammamet – few holidaymakers can resist buying a stuffed camel which range from the pocket-sized to those scarily close to full size. Equally cumbersome to carry home are decorative blue and white bird cages often seen in tourist hotel reception areas where they are used to collect letters and postcards.

Official Shops
ONAT/SOCOPA Shops

In the major tourist centres there is a chain of craft workshops and outlets run by the Organisation National de l'Artisanat Tunisien (ONAT or the National Organisation of Tunisian Craftsmen). The prices are fixed and may be higher than you could pay by haggling, but these shops are less hassle and the goods are generally fairly high quality. The stock tends to be very similar throughout the country, but local produce is always promoted. Opening hours are about 8.30–noon and 4–7pm, but may be shorter in smaller towns.

Bizerte
Quai Khémais Ternane, Old Port
Gabès
Avenue Farhat Hached
Houmt Souq
Avenue Bourguiba
El Jem
Avenue Farhat Hached
Monastir
Rue Abdessalem Trimeche
Nabeul
144 avenue Farhat Hached and 93 Habib Thameur
Sfax
10 rue Lt Hamadi Taj
Tunis
Le Palmarium, avenue Bourguiba

...and Haggle

Bargaining is a way of life throughout the Arab world and, with the notable exception of food and medicines, applies to most commercial transactions. As a general rule, do not express any interest in anything you do not really intend to buy, and always start at a figure that is roughly half of what you would actually be prepared to pay.

Most tourist towns have at least one official shop where prices are fixed (▶ left).

Children's Attractions

Children's Car Seats

Tunisia has no laws concerning the safety of children in cars which means that most rented vehicles and taxis will not have rear seatbelts. If you are concerned about this and planning to rent a car, you will need to inquire in advance. However the reality is that international firms are no more likely than local ones to be able to provide them and it is recommended that visitors take their own strap-in child seats.

Children in Tunisia

Children are assured of a warm welcome in Tunisia. As with many Mediterranean countries children are treated with affection, and in Tunisia latest figures show that more than 50 per cent of the people are under 18 while around one-third are under 14.

But visitors should be aware of the cultural differences which exist in attitudes towards young people. In Tunisia it is not unusual for children to work in shops and markets, to play unsupervised, ride on the back of motorbikes without any sort of protective headgear, and to hitch lifts from complete strangers. This can cause astonishment and concern to first-time European visitors.

They, in turn, can take offence when Tunisians begin fussing over their children, admiring them, occasionally touching them, complimenting the parents and asking what may seem like nosy questions. As always, the best advice is to be relaxed and diplomatic and to remember that half the reason for travelling is for it not to be like home.

Activities for children

Since Tunisia is still developing its package tourism industry there are very few attractions aimed specifically at children such as theme parks and adventure playgrounds. Most museums are not even adult-friendly let alone geared to the minds of children. So most families tend to stick to the beach resorts as children will prefer playing in the sand and sea than touring Roman ruins or walking round *souqs* and markets. However, the list below gives information on some places designed specifically for children.

Hammamet
Carthageland

Small zoo, attractions explaining the story of Barbarossa and other stories, a model of a Phoenician boat, as well as an area for smaller children.

✉ rue de la Medina, Yasmine Hammamet ☎ 72 240111 www.carthageland.com.tn

🕐 Daily

Djerba
Djerba Explore

The town's newest attraction park with a small but very good Islamic museum, a crocodile farm and a heritage museum.

✉ Route Touristique de Midoun - BP 353. Midoun ☎ 75 745277; www.djerbaexplore.com

🕐 Summer daily 9–8; winter daily 9–6

Port El Kantaoui
Acqua Palace

This waterpark is modest in scale, but it offers a large swimming pool, waterslides, wave machine and a paddling pool.

✉ 9km north of Sousse ☎ 73 348855 🕐 Daily 9.30–6 On-site pizzeria, self-service restaurant and bar

Tunis
Zoo du Belvédère

This small zoo houses a selection of wild cats, birds, snakes and camels.

✉ Park Belvédère ☎ 71 281846 🕐 9–7 (9–4 in winter)

Buses, camel rides and water taxis

In Hammamet, Sousse, Port El Kantaoui and Monastir, so-called 'Noddy Trains' – open-sided tourist shuttle buses – are always popular with small children as are short camel rides which are available on many beaches. Watersports are always popular with children and many resort hotels offer tuition for pursuits such as windsurfing. Taking a picnic to another beach by water taxi or making an excursion in a glass-bottomed boat to look at the underwater life is always a popular option.

Pools and playgrounds

One of the reasons Tunisia has become so popular as a beach destination is that it offers long, warm, sunny days, safe seas and clean beaches making it well suited to families. Many of the bigger hotels have separate children's pools and playgrounds. Some also provide children's clubs with qualified staff arranging day-long organised activities. In addition, some hotels offer child discounts or will put a child's bed in an adult's room free of charge.

Food and drink

Do not expect to find children's menus except in tourist hotels; normally they will be expected to eat a smaller portion of the adult meal. In resorts, there should be no problems finding hamburgers, hot dogs or pizzas. Pasta dishes also feature prominently on many menus, and the usual fizzy drinks, such as cola and lemonade, are widely available. Some children may find Tunisian dishes too spicy, particularly those containing the fiery *harissa* sauce made from chillies. You can always ask for dishes to be 'sans piquant', but this is not always possible. Salads are often a safe choice as they are invariably based around tuna or eggs. Most children will also enjoy the sticks of crispy white bread which accompany any meal or save up their appetite for a honey-soaked pastry like *baklava* or *makroud*. Finding provisions for a picnic can be a challenge as most supermarkets stock a limited range, but markets are where most Tunisians shop and there is always a vast choice of food.

Necessities for babies

Small-size disposable nappies are available at all chemists, although the larger sizes (over 15kg) can be difficult to find. You are not likely to experience problems in finding dried baby milk or bottled and tinned baby food.

Sun precautions

Remember that the sun is extremely strong in Tunisia, particularly in the summer months. Apply plenty of sunblock and insist children wear wide-brimmed hats, particularly if going on a boat trip: the cooling influence of the wind can be misleading, and the reflective effect of the water makes the rays even more powerful. Make sure you have a dense parasol for the pram if you are taking a baby along.

Public Toilets

There are very few public toilets in Tunisia except at railway stations and airports and these may not be up to the standard usually found in Europe and North America. The best bet is to head to the nearest café or restaurant. Always carry toilet paper as it is rarely supplied. Hand-cleaning wipes can also come in useful.

Sport

Flying Falcons
El Haouaria in the Cap Bon region is Tunisia's main falconry centre. Local enthusiasts catch young peregrine falcons and sparrowhawks in March and April and train them up for an annual Falconry Festival in mid-June. The Club des Fauconniers provides very helpful information for those interested in falconry. Located just outside El Haouaria, it is open from 10–4 daily.

Diving
Tunisia is steadily gaining recognition as a leading scuba-diving destination. The strongest interest is centred on Tabarka which has three major diving sites: Cap Tabarka, Grouper Rock and Tunnels Reef, which is an extraordinary complex of tunnels, caverns, caves and gullies.

Tabarka
Aquamarin
☎ 78 673508

École de Plongée
☎ 78 644344

Mehari Diving Centre
☎ 78 673136

Yachting Club de Tabarka
☎ 78 671478

Diving is also available at the Port el Kantouai resort, accessible by bus from Sousse (▶ 70).

Fishing
There is no river fishing in Tunisia but plenty of sea fishing is available. No permit is required and most harbours have boats for hire with or without crew.

Football
Football is the country's national sport and obsession, and is a useful opening conversational gambit with any Tunisian alike. All over the country there are organised matches on Sunday afternoons. Tunisia also has its own football league. In Tunis, two local teams – Espérance Sportif and Club Africain – share the El Menzah ground at Cité Olympique.

Golf
Tunisia's temperate year-round climate provides ideal golfing conditions. Many first-time visitors are often surprised by the golf courses in Tunisia which are generally lush and well maintained. A former golf-loving minister of tourism was partly responsible for persuading the government to invest heavily in the sport to provide an added attraction for holidaymakers. Most of the big resorts now have international standard courses. There are no membership requirements and while golfers with their own kit are welcome, those who prefer to travel light will find that everything from clubs to caddies are available for hire – all at very reasonable rates. Many hotels will organise pre-set tee-times and provide complimentary transport to and from courses.

Hammamet
Golf Citrus
Designed and landscaped with six lakes, olive trees and forest, Golf Citrus comprises two 18-hole 72-par championship courses. There is also a schooling course, driving range and putting greens.
✉ **Bir Bou Rebka, 13km west of Hammamet** ☎ **72 226500 Fax 72 226400**

Golf Yasmine
Golf Yasmine is a more intimate course adjacent to Golf Citrus. It offers a single 18-hole course, constructed around twin lakes.
✉ **Bir Bou Rebka, 13km west of Hammamet** ☎ **72 227001 Fax 72 226722**

Port El Kantaoui
El Kantaoui Golf Course
A 36-hole course particularly popular in November, February and March.

✉ **Opposite the Hotel Green Park** ☎ **73 231755 Fax 73 348755**

Skanès
Palm Links Golf Course
Ideally suited to beginners, an 18-hole, 72-par course with a nine-hole schooling course and driving range.

✉ **Dkhila** ☎ **73 466910 Fax 73 466913**

Tunis
Carthage Golf Course
Tunisia's oldest golf club, established in 1927, provides an 18-hole, 66-par course.

✉ **Choutrana 2, La Soukra** ☎ **71 765919 Fax 71 765915**

Horse riding
There are horses for hire on most tourist beaches and a few coastal hotels even have their own stables. Jerba is particularly well supplied with horses and ponies, and prices are very reasonable. In the Tunis area lessons and escorted rides are available.

Tunis
Club Hippique de la Soukra
✉ **La Soukra, 15km north of Tunis** ☎ **71 203054**

Hunting
The shooting season (Dec–Feb) is centred on the Khroumir Mountains around Ain Draham and Tabarka. The main prey are jackals, foxes, mongooses and wild boar. Permits are necessary and can be arranged by hotels, but it's best to organise these through a tour operator before arrival.

Sailing
Tunisia has some of the best marinas in North Africa which attract wealthy Europeans in the summer and 'yachties' from all over the world in the winter. Facilities are generally high quality and security good. Marinas can be found at:

Bizerte
El Kantaoui
Monastir
Sidi Bou Saïd
Tabarka
Tunis (La Goulette)

Swimming
All major beach hotels have at least one swimming pool, and many now offer indoor pools to attract winter guests. Even if you are not staying in a hotel it is usually possible to use the pool for a small charge. Sea swimming is usually safe and pleasant but jellyfish can be a problem in some areas.

Tennis
Most tennis courts in Tunisia are attached to beach hotels and can usually be used by outside guests as well as residents. Some of the most extensive facilities are at the Club Mediterranée resorts in Jerba and Monastir – but these are closed to non-residents.

Tunis
Cap Carthage
A 30-court complex.

✉ **15km northeast of Tunis** ☎ **71 740064**

Walking
Ain Draham, Le Kef, Tamerza and Zaghouan are among the main hill-walking centres in Tunisia.

Watersports
One of Tunisia's biggest attractions as a beach destination is that all its major beach resorts are well-equipped with a wide variety of watersports facilities. From hiring a pedalo to more energetic pursuits such as windsurfing, waterskiing, sailing and paragliding, facilities and equipment are available at very reasonable rates. Hammamet alone has more than more than a dozen watersports centres.

Nightlife

Bars

Outside of the main tourist hotels, drinking in most Tunisian bars is confined to early evenings, from around 6 to 9pm. Grimy and smoky, the bars are a meeting place as much as anything else; men of all ages sit together playing cards, smoking *chichas* (through a water pipe) and drinking beer.

The range of night-time entertainment on offer in Tunisia is quite limited. Outside the capital, most evening activities are centred around the tourist hotels, many of which provide free entertainment several times a week. This generally involves local musicians playing easy-listening, inter-nationally known songs – which, after all, is probably what most tourists want after a long day spent in the sun.

Most tour operators will also offer holidaymakers the opportunity to book an evening excursion to a local nightspot for a 'Tunisian Evening' where a specially tailored version of a traditional Tunisian meal is provided – served with generous amounts of wine and beer. The entertainment on offer normally comprises young women in silk robes and head-dresses performing traditional dances to the accompaniment of folk music. Sometimes there will also be a juggler, snake charmer or belly-dancer – although it is rare to see a performance by a genuine belly-dancer.

Cabaret Dinners

Tunis
El Mawel
✉ rue Amine Abbassi
☎ 71 790321 🕐 Nightly

El Mazar
Live music in a cosy atmosphere with a mix of local people and tourists.
✉ rue de Marseille (above La Mamma restaurant) ☎ 71 340423 🕐 Nightly from 6–8.30

M'rabet
Quite touristic, which is reflected in the mediocre food, but the décor is beautiful, but the location as central as it gets, and it's a great place for afternoon mint tea. Folkloric show at night with Berber dancing, belly dancing and traditional Moorish music.
✉ Souk et Trouk, Medina
☎ 71 561729 🕐 Lunch, dinner. Closed Sun

La Privé
✉ rue de l'Abrabie Saoudite
☎ 71 891633

Nightclubs

Bizerte
Hôtel Corniche Palace
✉ rue de la Corniche
☎ 72 421222

Hôtel Jalta
✉ route de la Corniche
☎ 72 443100

Hammamet
Cotton Club
✉ avenue Moncef Bey
☎ 72 227053

Calypso
✉ avenue Moncef Bey
☎ 72 226803

Habana Club
✉ route Touristique
☎ no phone

Manhattan
✉ Hammamet Sud
☎ 72 226226

Le Pacha
✉ avenue Moncef Bey
☎ 72 226462

Tropicana
✉ route Touristique
☎ 72 227200

Mahdia
Club Cesar
✉ Hôtel Thapsus, Zone
Touristique ☎ 73 694495

Samba
✉ Hôtel Mehdi, Zone
Touristique ☎ 73 671287

Skanès
Hôtel Kuriat Palace
✉ Zone touristique
☎ 73 521200

Hôtel Sahara Beach
✉ Zone Touristique
☎ 73 461088

Sousse
King Nightclub
✉ Hôtel Samara, boulevard
Abdelhami Kadhi ☎ 72 226699

Maracana
✉ Hôtel Tej Marhaba
☎ 73 229800

Tabarka
**Hôtel Abou Nawas
Montazah**
✉ route Touristique
☎ 78 673532

Tunis
Club 2001
✉ Abou Nawas El Mechtel,
avenue Ouled Haffouz ☎ 71
780450

JFK
✉ Oscars Hotel, 12–14 rue de
Marseille ☎ 71 345558

Casinos
Casinos have only recently
been recognised as another
way of attracting tourists and
are at present few and far
between, but new ones are
being built all the time. To
gain entry you will need to
be over 21 and non-Muslim,
so take your passport.

Since it is forbidden to
gamble with Tunisian dinars,
you will need US dollars or
some other form of hard
currency. Travellers'
cheques, Eurocheques
and credit cards are also
accepted. Opening hours
are usually noon–4am,
and the dress code is
smart casual.

Hammamet
Casino Emeraude
✉ boulevard Assad ibn el
Fourat ☎ 72 278655

Grand Casino
✉ Sol Azur Beach Hotel, route
Touristique, Hammamet North
☎ 72 240777

Jerba
Grand Casino
✉ Sidi Mehrez ☎ 75 757537

Sousse
Casino Club Caraïbe
✉ boulevard 7 Novembre
☎ 73 211777

Cinemas
Cinemas are found all over
the country and are one of
the most popular forms of
entertainment in Tunisia.
With only a tiny film-making
industry of its own, the
cinemas rely largely on a
programme of violent
American films, kung fu
movies and Arabic films,
mainly from Egypt.
In Tunis there are more than
20 cinemas, including one at
the Hôtel l'Africa (▶ 101)
which sometimes shows
more highbrow French
language films. Matinées
usually start at 3pm with
evening performances at
6pm and 9pm.

Hammams
One of the most leisurely
ways of spending an
evening or afternoon is by
visiting a *hammam* – a
traditional steam bath.
Found all over Tunisia and
popular since Roman
times, most Tunisians will
visit a *hammam* at least
once a week, not only for
relaxation and cleanliness
but as a place to meet and
chat. Visitors keen to learn
more about the Tunisians
will find a visit to a
hammam very rewarding.
Avoid hotel *hammams*
which are a travesty of the
real thing.

What's On When

Ramadan

Ramadan is by far the most important festival in any Muslim country and is adhered to by the vast majority of Tunisians. The Koran demands that during the month-long festival (the date of which varies from year to year) no water and no food must pass a Muslim's lips during daylight hours. Some tourists avoid travelling to Muslim countries during Ramadan but it can be quite an exciting time as each evening eating and drinking continue into the early hours. The end of Ramadan is marked with a massive celebration – the Aid es Seghir.

As a Muslim country, Tunisia celebrates a number of national festivals related to Islam, including the month-long fast of Ramadan (▶ panel). The dates of these religious events are calculated according to the Muslim calendar which is lunar. Dates are thus 11 days earlier each year. Aid el Adha is a celebration of Abraham's devotion to God who told him to sacrifice his son, but 'stayed his hand' when He saw that Abraham was prepared to do so. A sheep is killed and the family feast. *Mouled* is a celebration of the Prophet Muhammad's birthday, and Al-Hijra is the Muslim New Year.

The following are among the most popular local festivals:

February

Olive Festival: Kalaa Kebira (near Sousse).

March–April

Ksour Festival: Berber traditions and folklore, Tataouine.
Orange Blossom Festival: cultural events, Nabeul and Menzel Bouzelta.

May

Tuna Harvest: Matanza Sidi Daoud in Cap Bon. Tuna caught en masse on their annual migration.

June

Falconry Festival: falcons trained by villagers take part in a series of competitions to catch partridge and quail before being released into the wild. El Haouaria.
Ulysses Festival: folklore festival including a re-enactment of the arrival in Jerba of Ulysses, Jerba.

July–August

Festival of Carthage: the biggest cultural festival in Tunisia. Staged in the restored Roman theatre at Carthage and including dance, film, theatre and musical events.
Classical Music Festival: El Jem.
Music Festival: week-long festival of *maalouf* music which was exported to North Africa by Andalusian refugees between the 12th and the 15th centuries. Testour (75km southwest of Tunis).
Dougga Festival: theatrical performances in the spectacular setting of the Roman theatre within the archaeological site, Dougga.
Festival of Theatre: folk music, dancing and plays, Sousse.
International Jazz Festival: Tabarka.
Jerba Folklore Festival: held every other year (even years), Jerba.
International Festival: music, dance and theatre, Monastir.

September

Cavalry Festival: displays of horsemanship, Kairouan.

November

Date Harvest Festival: Kebili.
Festival of Tozeur: oasis folklore and traditions, Tozeur.
International Film Festival: held bi-annually (even years), Carthage.

December

International Festival of the Sahara: attracts up to 50,000 Bedouin, nomads and tourists for camel races and folklore displays. Held on the edge of town, Douz.

Practical Matters

Above: *Tunis has an efficient metro system*
Right: *A decorative postbox in Hammamet*

GMT	Tunisia	Germany	USA (NY)	Netherlands	Spain
12 noon	1PM	1 PM	7AM	1PM	1PM

BEFORE YOU GO

WHAT YOU NEED

		UK	GERMANY	USA	Netherlands	Spain
● Required ○ Suggested ▲ Not required	Some countries require a passport to remain valid for a minimum period (usually at least six months) beyond the date of entry – contact their consulate or embassy or your travel agent for details.					
Passport		●	●	●	●	●
Visa (regulations can change – check before booking your trip)		▲	▲	▲	▲	▲
Onward or Return Ticket		▲	▲	▲	▲	▲
Health Inoculations		○	○	○	○	○
Health Documentation (► 123, Health)		▲	▲	▲	▲	▲
Travel Insurance		●	●	●	●	●
Driving Licence (national or international)		●	●	●	●	●
Car Insurance Certificate (if own car)		●	●	●	●	●
Car Registration Document (if own car)		●	●	●	●	●

WHEN TO GO

Tunis

■■■■■ High season
▢ Low season

16°C	17°C	20°C	21°C	23°C	27°C	30°C	32°C	29°C	25°C	22°C	17°C
JAN	FEB	MAR	APR	MAY	JUN	JUL	AUG	SEP	OCT	NOV	DEC

🌧 Very wet   🌧 Wet   ☀ Sun   ⛅ Sunshine/Showers

TOURIST OFFICES

In the UK
Tunisian National Tourist Office
77A Wigmore Street
London W1H 9LJ
☎ 020 7224 5598
Fax: 020 7224 4053
www.tourismtunisia.co.uk

In the USA
C/o Ambassade de Tunisie
1515 Massachusetts Ave
NW
Washington DC 20005
☎ (202) 466 2546
Fax: (202) 862 1858

In France
Office National du
Tourisme Tunisien
32 avenue de l'Opera,
Paris 75002
☎ (33-1) 4742-7267
email: ONTT@wanadoo.fr

WHEN YOU ARE THERE

ARRIVING

There are two major gateways. Tunis-Carthage International Airport handles scheduled flights from all over Europe. (There are no direct services from the US). Tunisia's domestic airline TunInter operates flights to Jerba, Tozeur and Sfax. Monastir-Skanès International Airport is used by charter flights.

Tunis-Carthage International Airport

9 kilometres

Journey times

🚌	20–25 minutes
🚍	12 minutes

Monastir-Skanès International Airport

5 kilometres

Journey times

🚌	20 minutes
🚍	10 minutes
🚗	15 minutes

MONEY

The monetary unit of Tunisia is the dinar which is divided into 1,000 millimes. There is a one dinar coin and coins for 5, 10, 20, 50, 100 and 500 mills. Banknotes come in 5D, 10D and 20D denominations. The dinar is a 'soft' currency which means that exchange rates are fixed artificially by the government and cannot be traded on world currency markets. It is illegal to import or export dinars so you will be unable to obtain local currency in advance.

TIME

🕐 Tunisia is one hour ahead of GMT all year round which means that flying from Britain in summer there is no time difference while in winter watches have to be put forward one hour.

CUSTOMS

→ YES

Alcohol:	spirits 1L
Still table wine:	2L
Cigarettes:	200 or
Cigars:	40 or
Tobacco:	400gms
Perfume:	50ml
Toilet water:	1L
Cameras:	2
Video camera:	1

10 rolls of black & white film and 20 rolls of colour
Jewellery with a precious content: up to 500 grms.
Musical instrument: 1
A car, motorcycle, caravan or boat.

⊖ NO

Drugs, firearms, ammunition, offensive weapons, obscene material, unlicensed animals.

119

EMBASSIES AND CONSULATES

UK	USA	Germany	Netherlands	Spain
☎ 71 108700	☎ 71 107000	☎ 71 786455	☎ 070 351 2251	☎ 71 782217
		Fax: 01 788242		Fax: 01 786267

WHEN YOU ARE THERE

TOURIST OFFICES

Bizerte
✉ quai Khemais Ternane, Old Port
☎ 72 432897

Hammamet
✉ avenue de la Répulic
☎ 72 280423

Jerba
✉ boulevard de l'Environnement
☎ 75 650016

Monastir
✉ Zone Touristique de Skanès
☎ 73 520205

Nabeul
✉ avenue Taïeb Mehri
☎ 72 286800
www.nabeul.net

Sousse
✉ 1 avenue Habib Bourguiba
☎ 73 225157

Tabarka
✉ avenue 7 Novembre
☎ 78 673555

Tozeur
✉ 89 avenue Abdul Kacem Chabbi
☎ 76 454503
Fax: 76 452051

Tunis
✉ 1 avenue Mohamed V
☎ 71 341077

www.tourismtunisia.com

NATIONAL HOLIDAYS

J	F	M	A	M	J	J	A	S	O	N	D
1	0	2	1	1	0	1	1	0	1	1	0

1 January	New Year's Day
20 March	Independence Day
21 March	Youth Day
9 April	Martyrs' Day
1 May	International Labour Day
25 July	Republic Day
13 August	Women's Day
15 October	Evacuation of Bizerte
7 November	Anniversary of the Events of 1987

In addition to these secular holidays there are also various Muslim feast days which follow the Gregorian calendar and move backwards by roughly 11 days a year. The biggest holiday is the three-day feast called Aid es-Seghir, marking the end of Ramadan.

OPENING HOURS

○ Shops ● Museums
● Restaurants (lunch) ○ Post offices
● Banks ○ Pharmacies

9 AM	10 AM	11 AM	12 PM	1 PM	2 PM	3 PM	4 PM	5 PM	6 PM
9.30	10.30	11.30	12.30	1.30	2.30	3.30	4.30	5.30	

Opening hours can be flexible according to region, time of year and even individual whims. In summer it is not unusual for shops to stay closed for much of the afternoon and then re-open again in the evening when it is cooler. During Ramadan working hours are also generally shortened all round. Many museums and archaeological sites are closed on Mondays. Pharmacies are found in every village and are generally clean and well-stocked with staff speaking fluent French. In large towns, there will be a pharmacy open 24 hours a day, but closed Sundays.

**DRIVE ON THE
RIGHT**

**TOILETS
BASIC**

★ ★
★ ★

PUBLIC TRANSPORT

 Internal Flights Tunisia's relatively small size means there is not much demand for domestic air travel. The two busiest routes are between Tunis and Tozeur and Tunis and Jerba which is used as a major gateway into Libya. All internal flights are operated by TunInter.

 Trains Tunisia's small but efficient rail network is operated by the Societé Nationale des Chemins de Fer Tunisiens (SNCFT). The main line runs north to south from Tunis to Gabes. Three trains daily, whole route; eight services from Tunis to Sousse, six from Tunis to Sfax. Trains offer three classes – second, first and *confort*. Some have air-conditioned carriages.

Buses There is a wide network of bus routes operated by a variety of companies. Bigger towns usually have a central bus station called the *gare routière*. Local buses are usually filled to the brim, especially on market days when you may find yourself sharing the journey with chickens or sheep.

Ferries The busiest ferries in Tunisia are those operating between Jorf and Ajim on the island of Jerba. There are year-round services between Tunis and the Italian ports of Genoa and Trapani, with summer connections between Tunis and Naples. Compagnie Tunisienne de Navigation (01 346572) operates between Tunis and Marseille.

Urban Transport Tunis has a *metro leger* (tram) network and a very limited suburban rail service connecting the capital with Carthage and La Marsa. Services are punctual if not exactly frequent. There is also a metro service between Sousse and Maholia which is particularly useful for holidaymakers staying at hotels in Skanès.

CAR RENTAL

 Car rental in Tunisia is expensive. Even vehicles from international rental companies can be poorly maintained, and there are many potential hazards, from people driving at night without lights to pedestrians walking out into the road without looking.

TAXIS

 Official taxis are yellow and equipped with a meter. Some drivers will try not to use it, in which case insist, fix a fare in advance or get out and use another taxi. There is a 50% surcharge between 9pm and 6am. In several resorts you can also hire *calèches*.

DRIVING

 Speed limit on motorways: **110kph**

 Speed limit on main roads: **90kph**

 Speed limit in built-up areas: **50kph**

 Seat belts are compulsory for the driver and front-seat passenger on roads between cities but are rarely used.

 Random Breath Testing: No breath-testing but there are a lot of traffic police and local people are regularly asked to produce their papers. It is almost unheard of for a tourist to be booked unless they cause an accident.

 Petrol: Fuel is cheap by European standards and costs the same everywhere. It is sold as super, regular and *essence sans plomb* (lead-free petrol). Although petrol stations are reasonably plentiful, never make the mistake of running short on fuel especially when driving in more remote areas.

 Breakdown: Do not expect to be able to call a motoring assistance organisation – although some of the major international car rental companies will provide replacement vehicles and help. Garage mechanics can normally fix most problems. Punctured tyres are common, so if planning a long journey take food and blankets.

PERSONAL SAFETY

Tunisia is a very safe country with a relatively low crime rate. Sadly, petty thieving is on the increase particularly in busy resorts. Beware of groups of small children distracting you with posies of flowers or cheap souvenirs. To reduce the risk of theft or assault:

- Beware of pickpockets, especially in crowded markets and *souqs*.
- Keep cameras and other valuables in closed bags.
- Do not carry more money and valuables than you need.
- Make use of hotel safes.
- Do not walk alone around *médinas* at night.
- Women should dress modestly, covering themselves when away from the beach or hotel.

Police assistance:
☎ **197** from any call box

TELEPHONES

Tunisia's telephone system is quite efficient. In most places you can dial direct on a coin phone at the post office or from one of the many Taxiphone or Publitel offices. There will be several booths under one roof with an attendant to give change. You can make a direct dial international call very easily using one dinar coins or use a phonecard. Some shops selling phonecards have public phones, usually indicated by a blue sign.

International Dialling Codes from Tunisia to:

UK:	00 44
Germany:	00 49
USA and Canada:	00 1
Netherlands:	00 31

POST

Post offices are known as PTTs (Poste, Telephone, Telegraph) and are well-represented throughout the country. They sell stamps – although these can also be bought from hotels, newsagents and kiosks. Postboxes are generally small and yellow. Postcards and letters to Europe can take about a week to arrive.

ELECTRICITY

The voltage is 220/240v.

The power supply in Tunisia is 220 volts although a few more remote areas are still on 110 volts. Sockets accept two-round pin plugs so an international adaptor is needed for most non-continental European appliances. A transformer is needed for appliances operating on 100-120 volts.

TIPS/GRATUITIES

Yes ✓	No ✗	
Restaurants (if service not included)	✓	10%
Cafes/bars (if service not included)	✓	A few coins
Tour guide	✓	
Hairdressers	✗	
Taxis	✓	Optional
Chambermaids	✓	A few coins
Hotel porters	✓	(500mills to TD1)
Theatre/cinema usherettes)	✗	
Cloakroom attendants	✓	(a small coin)
Toilets	✓	Optional

PHOTOGRAPHY

What to photograph: Busy market scenes, the dramatic desert landscape, Sidi Bou Said, camels, mosques, archaeological sites.

What not to photograph: Government buildings, people in uniform, anything military, airports, the Tunisian flag.

When to photograph: Very early morning and early evening.

Where to buy film: It is probably best to bring as much film as you think you will need although most major brands are available from camera shops and souvenir kiosks.

HEALTH

Insurance
Do not try to skimp on travel insurance, which is well worth the investment should problems occur. If you fall ill, all major tourist hotels or a pharmacist should be able to recommend a good doctor – although any treatment would have to be paid for and then reclaimed. If you end up in hospital, immediately contact your insurance company which is there to provide support and advice.

Dental Services
Most tourist hotels should be able to recommend a reputable dentist. Any treatment will need to be paid for and then reclaimed on insurance. It is advised to have a thorough dental check-up before leaving home.

Sun Advice
The sun in Tunisia can be very hot, particularly between June and September in the main beach resorts and in the deep south. Wear a hat, loose cotton clothing and a high factor sunscreen. Drink plenty of bottled water, avoid excess alcohol and caffeine as these aid dehydration – and restrict the amount of time spent in direct sunlight.

Drugs
Pharmacists are knowledgeable and well-respected in Tunisia. Their shops are generally well-supplied although it is always worth checking the date stamp on any medicines which can deteriorate quickly in the heat. Pharmacists can supply drugs for many minor complaints such as sore throat, upset stomach or diarrhoea. Never buy illegal drugs.

CONCESSIONS

Students/Youths: Students with valid identification may get reductions at historical sights and museums. There is a small network of youth hostels in Tunisia, five of them run by the country's Youth Hostel Association. Clean and cheap, there is strict segregation between men and women and an 11pm curfew is imposed. In theory you need to produce a relevant membership card – but it is not always asked for.

Senior Citizens: Tunisia is a very popular destination with older travellers – although they receive no special discounts. Senior citizens tend to be more respected by society than they are in many western countries. It is not unusual for several generations of a family to live together and there is generally much greater interaction between young and old.

CLOTHING SIZES

Tunisia	UK	Rest of Europe	USA	
46	36	46	36	
48	38	48	38	
50	40	50	40	Suits
52	42	52	42	
54	44	54	44	
56	46	56	46	
41	7	41	8	
42	7.5	42	8.5	
43	8.5	43	9.5	Shoes
44	9.5	44	10.5	
45	10.5	45	11.5	
46	11	46	12	
37	14.5	37	14.5	
38	15	38	15	
39/40	15.5	39/40	15.5	Shirts
41	16	41	16	
42	16.5	42	16.5	
43	17	43	17	
34	8	34	6	
36	10	36	8	
38	12	38	10	Dresses
40	14	40	12	
42	16	42	14	
44	18	44	16	
38	4.5	38	6	
38	5	38	6.5	
39	5.5	39	7	Shoes
39	6	39	7.5	
40	6.5	40	8	
41	7	41	8.5	

WHEN DEPARTING

- There are no airport taxes, but you should exchange your spare dinars at the airport as it is illegal to export Tunisian currency. Have your exchange slips with you as you are only allowed to reconvert up to 30 per cent of the total amount of money exchanged in Tunisia.
- Tunisia's airports can be very busy in the summer so allow plenty of time to check-in for your homeward flight.

LANGUAGE

Tunisia is almost bilingual. Although the official language is Arabic, nearly everyone speaks some French and increasingly common among wealthier classes and the business community is for people to speak 'Frarabic'– a rather odd mixture of the two. Not content with two languages under their belt, a lot of young Tunisians are also learning English or German. Tourists can do their bit by learning a few words of Arabic, which is well worth the effort as it usually brings instant friendship.

	hotel	un hôtel	otel/fondouk
	I want a room	Je voudrais une chambre	B'gheet beet
	Can I look at it?	Est-ce qu'on peut la voir	Yoomkin ashoofa?
	How much?	Combien?	Kaddésh?
	too expensive	c'est trop	yessir
	shower	la douche	doosha
	open	ouvert	mahoul
	closed	ferme	msaker
	bank	une banque	bank
	post office	une poste	bousta/barid
	1, 2, 3, 4, 5	une, deux, trois, quatre, cinq	wahed, jooj, tlata, arba, khamsa
	6, 7, 8, 9, 10	six, sept, huit, neuf, dix	setta, seba, tmenia, tse'ud, a'chra
	100, 1000	cent, mille	mia, alf
	the bill	l'addition	el-hisaab
	fish	poisson	samak/hoot
	meat	viande	lahm
	vegetables	légumes	khodra
	fruit	fruit	fawakih
	water	de l'eau	maa
	soup	potage	shorba
	coffee	café	kahwa
	tea	thé	shay
	wine	vin	sharab
	bread	pain	khoubz
	airport	l'aéroport	al-matar
	bus	l'autobus	autobees
	car	la voiture	sayara
	train station	gare	mahata el tren
	garage	le garage	garage
	petrol	l'essence	benzeen
	puncture	le crevaison	tokob
	yes	oui	naam
	no	non	la'a
	please	s'il vous plaît	birabee
	thank you	merci	shukran
	hello	bonjour	aslémah
	good morning	bonjour	sabah el khir
	good evening	bon soir	missa el khir
	goodbye	au revoir	bislémah
	excuse me	pardon	samahnee
	how are you?	ça va?	ashnooa ahwalik?

INDEX

Acknowledgements
The Automobile Association wishes to thank the following photographers and libraries for their assistance in the preparation of this book.
THE J ALLAN CASH PHOTOLIBRARY 39, 57c; BRUNO BARBY/MAGNUM PHOTOS 14b; MARY EVANS PICTURE LIBRARY 10b, 14c; INTERNATIONAL PHOTOBANK 8c, 91b; MRI BANKERS' GUIDE TO FOREIGN CURRENCY 119; ROBERT HARDING PICTURE LIBRARY 21; SPECTRUM COLOUR LIBRARY 51b, 52b, 73b, 79b; TUNISIA NATIONAL TOURIST OFFICE 9b, 87a; WORLD PICTURES LIBRARY LTD 61.

The remaining photographs are held in the Automobile Assocation's own library (AA PHOTO LIBRARY) and were taken by Steve Day.

Peter Lilley would like to thank Ann Noon of the Tunisian National Tourist Office, London; Jason Nicholls, GB Airways; Panorama Holidays; Abou Nawas Hotels.

Updated by Sylvie Franquet